THE ANIMAL RESEARCH WAR

THE ANIMAL RESEARCH WAR

P. Michael Conn

James V. Parker

THE ANIMAL RESEARCH WAR

First published in 2008 by
PALGRAVE MACMILLAN™
175 Fifth Avenue, New York, N.Y. 10010 and
Houndmills, Basingstoke, Hampshire, England RG21 6XS.
Companies and representatives throughout the world.

PALGRAVE MACMILLAN is the global academic imprint of the Palgrave Macmillan division of St. Martin's Press, LLC and of Palgrave Macmillan Ltd. Macmillan® is a registered trademark in the United States, United Kingdom and other countries. Palgrave is a registered trademark in the European Union and other countries.

ISBN-13: 978-0-230-60014-0
ISBN-10: 0-230-60014-X

Library of Congress Cataloging-in-Publication Data

Conn, P. Michael.
    The animal research war / P. Michael Conn, James V. Parker.
    p. cm.
    Includes bibliographical references and index.
    ISBN 0-230-60014-X
    1. Animal experimentation—Moral and ethical aspects—United States. 2. Animal welfare—Moral and ethical aspects—United States. 3. Animal rights—United States. 4. Animal rights movement—United States. I. Parker, James V. II. Title.

HV4915.C66 2008
179.4—dc22   2007041199

A catalogue record of the book is available from the British Library.

Design by Scribe Inc.

First edition: May 2008

10 9 8 7 6 5 4 3 2 1

Printed in the United States of America.

CONTENTS

Foreword   vii

Preface and Guide to Words   xi

1   In the Crosshairs   1

2   War Stories   11

3   The Animal Rights Movement Past and Present   41

4   Animal Rights Strategies   63

5   War Casualties   93

6   War Casualties: All of Us   107

7   Yes, but What About . . .   125

8   Peace at Last?   143

Appendix A: Twenty Questions   157

Appendix B: Resources   169

Notes   175

Works Cited   177

Index   191

FOREWORD

How would you feel if you had worked to advance human and animal health and well-being and yet were accused of doing evil? And what if that *untrue* accusation rooted and spread and then took on a life of its own, so that people knew you only by false reputation? Imagine a claim that for decades affected your family and friends, your colleagues, your career, and perhaps eventually your way of thinking and behaving.

Dr. Michael Conn has found himself in the crosshairs of a virulent campaign directed against biomedical researchers who use animals in their studies. Ironically, he hasn't personally conducted animal research for some twelve years—and then, only with rats and mice—but the fact that he is the Associate Director of the Oregon National Primate Research Center has made him a target of animal activists. Facts carry little weight in the minds of those who detest animal research: Conn is evil in their view, and they are free to use any tactic in their enormous arsenal of intimidation, lies, and harassment to derail him.

For the extreme fringe of the animal rights movement, achieving the goal of eliminating animal research justifies almost any tactic: recently, some have even said it would be acceptable to use violence against medical researchers who seek cures for the worst diseases, if that meant fewer animals would be used in research.

Even some so-called mainstream animal rights organizations that are not at the most violent fringe often cheer from the sidelines when a lab is destroyed, animals are stolen or released, or a researcher is so thoroughly intimidated that he or she gives in and gives up. They also supply intellectual and media cover and, sometimes, legal support for the hooded nightriders. And for them, as for their violent cousins, truth is elastic, to be stretched, twisted, and folded to just shy of the breaking point.

The fact is that biomedical research involving animals is a highly regulated process, controlled by federal and state legislation. For decades, most ethical researchers have subscribed to a pain-reduction philosophy dubbed "the 3 Rs" which the authors explain in this book. Today's scientific breakthroughs and tomorrow's treatments have come from research with animals—research that could not be accomplished in any other way, despite what the animal rights apologists may claim about computer models, *in vitro* testing, and other adjunct testing.

Michael Conn became engaged with the animal rights movement because *it* became obsessed with him. Along with his co-author, Dr. James Parker, who served eighteen years as Public Information Officer at the Oregon National Primate Research Center, when it was the subject of an infiltration by an individual working for an animal extremist group, Conn details the life of a targeted subject of the animal rights movement. In the meantime he has become an expert and consultant on the extremist mindset and on their methods that have been so effective in spreading falsehoods and doubt about animals in research.

In chapter after chapter, the authors unfold stories of attacks, from threats in the night, to baseball bat assaults, to the destruction of years of research. The authors also relate stories of individual bravery and, yes, even corporate strength in the face of threats to employees, customers, and suppliers. Equally, they explain the process of protecting animals in research and they put to rest some of the tired myths of laboratory animals—myths that animal extremists need to perpetuate in order to validate their own dire actions.

We hope you will read, learn from, and enjoy *The Animal Research War*. It is extremely important that an informed public know what is really going on and how it impacts on the future of health care and medical advances. We hope you will also pass it along and help spread truth.

*States United for Biomedical Research**

---

*States United for Biomedical Research, with nearly five hundred member organizations, is a network of nonprofit associations that have joined forces to promote health through science and education. Its purpose is to promote public understanding and increase appreciation of the value of biomedical research, including the humane care and use of research animals. Members include hospitals, health care systems, universities, voluntary health organizations, professional associations, and others in the research community.

PREFACE AND GUIDE TO WORDS

We wrote this book because we believe in ethical animal research. We believe in its benefits and in our obligations to perform it. We also believe in the humane care of animals. Benefits of animal research are everywhere we look. They are easy to see in longer life spans for humans and the virtual disappearance of scourges like polio, smallpox, and the bubonic plague. These have been brought about by improved nutrition, modern sanitation, more effective public health measures, earlier diagnosis, refined surgical procedures, and better immunization and medication. Ethical animal research has contributed mightily to all this. Looking to the future, it is also our best hope of defense against emerging and not-understood diseases, from bird flu, Ebola, and AIDS, to autism and Alzheimer's. Our pets and wildlife, too, benefit from biomedical discoveries and live longer and better lives.

Some would have you believe otherwise.

Although most Americans approve of ethical animal research, about three in ten of us disapprove of it (although that figure might be significantly lower if pollsters were to explain the regulations that protect animals in research before asking their approve/disapprove question). These people believe that animals have rights, including the right not to be
• used by humans for any purpose—whether for food, clothing, entertainment, sport, medical research, or even companionship. Many of them act on their beliefs, and their actions run the gamut from abstaining from animal foods and clothing, letter writing, and political organizing, to raiding laboratories and sabotaging businesses, stalking and assaulting persons, and even fire-bombing facilities.

Especially the latter, the "direct actions," are signs of a war. It is a war with spies, bombs, and casualties. Because the battlefield is widespread and because the "animal army" is clandestine and, quite intentionally, not organized under a command structure, the war often goes unnoticed. A researcher-casualty quietly surrenders, leaving no corpus for media examination. The true victims, those suffering with disease and their friends and relatives, are far enough from the battlefield that they don't recognize what is happening.

We regret having to use the word "war." Had we written this book twenty years earlier, it wouldn't have crossed our minds to describe the challenge of the animal rights movement to animal research as a war. Things were different then. Researchers still trusted in openness and dialogue. We at the Oregon National Primate Research Center (ONPRC) toured the local affiliate of People for the Ethical Treatment of Animals (PeTA) through our own research facility, and we met with its members to listen to their objections and concerns as well as to explain the purposes, methods, regulations, and benefits of animal research.

Some years later came the threatening letters, the posting of pictures of researchers and inaccurate, inflammatory descriptions of their work on the Internet; nighttime "visits" to homes of researchers; the mailing of letters to scientists in envelopes armed with razor blades; and stories from other places of vandalism, assault and bombing. Although the perpetrators of these acts were not always known, for our personal safety we had to begin limiting access to the facilities, monitoring photographs of animal housing, restricting our participation in public forums and debates, and deleting names and other identifying information of colleagues from public records.

What word other than "war" can we employ to describe what is happening to the enterprise of biomedical research? Attack? Assault? Siege? All the words that come to mind come from the battlefield.

This is distressing to us. The metaphor of war can be self-defeating. We are confident that in any open and civilized public-policy debate, scientists, even though they tend to be poor communicators of their endeavors, would prevail over their challengers. But what will happen if researchers, convinced that they are encircled by belligerents, retreat behind barricades and remain incommunicado? Research and its beneficiaries—that is, all of us—stand to lose.

Some argue that our concern is misplaced (O'Neill). They argue that animal extremists in the UK, where bombings and assaults have already occurred, are a handful at most. With a few of their leaders already sitting in jail, their influence wanes. Better that scientists concentrate on communicating the nature, purpose, methods, and successes of biomedical research.

In our view, a small group of extremists in a social movement can exercise an influence wholly disproportionate to their numbers. They are more successful than their moderate colleagues in drawing public attention to their cause. And, they are chillingly effective in causing casualties, whether institutional or personal. This book reports, sadly, the stories of enterprises that have been hobbled and of scientists, who, for reasons of personal and family security, have quit the field of health research.

We are convinced that scientists, despite the risks they incur, must speak out. More on that after some remarks on words and terms, in addition to "war," that we use in this book. Words have power, as will be evident when we discuss the animal rights campaign to change "pet" and "owner" to "companion animal" and "animal guardian," and researchers' efforts to tar all their challengers as "terrorists." At the end of this introduction we provide a guide to a short list of such words. For the moment, "animal welfare," "animal," "animal rights," and "extremism" merit special attention.

The definition of animal welfare, the position that the authors support, will become clear in the book. Animal rights refers to the belief that animals, like humans, have rights, and that among those rights is that of not being used by humans for any purpose, no matter how noble. Animals are not meant to be our food, clothing, entertainment, sport, research subjects, or pets.

Extremism may seem to be a subjective term; what is extreme to me may be moderate to you. When we refer to animal extremists, we are thinking of those who would impose their views of what we should eat or wear or use through actions, sometimes legal but often illegal, that are meant to at least intimidate us. Extremists go beyond the civil disobedience that we respect in the actions of Mahatma Gandhi or Rosa Parks or Martin Luther King. Those heroes, who disobeyed what they considered to be unjust laws, disarmed their opponents in their willingness to suffer the painful consequences of openly following their consciences. Extremists, on the other hand, appear unwilling to pay the price of their convictions and thus operate behind masks and under the cloak of night. They seek not to change but to terrorize the hearts of their opponents.

All animal extremists, then, are animal rightists, but not all rightists are extremists. Here's a simple test to help distinguish which is which: animal extremists may be impatient with their fellow animal rightists, but they will never disown them. They claim to speak for rightists; in turn, they depend on the animal rights doctrine to justify their actions.

Many animal rightists, on the other hand, will publicly distance themselves from extremists. Some are appalled by violence, verbal or physical, and they fear that anything having the feel of terrorism turns ordinary folks against their cause. Others weasel: they proclaim that they reject violence, but then they allow that they "understand" and "sympathize" with those who practice it.

Turning from the subject of this book to us, the authors, another distinction bears mentioning. The "I" on these pages is Michael Conn, the scientist. His personal experiences in the last decade, identified by the first person singular, gave rise to the idea and structure of this book. Woven into and occasionally adding to his account is the voice of his colleague, James Parker, who comments in more general ways from years of tracking the animal rights movement.

Careers and lives develop unpredictably. The two of us now look back and ask, "Who, twenty years ago, would have believed what has happened to us, or could have predicted the situation in which research institutions now find themselves?" But it is not enough to just register our astonishment. We humans, like all animals, must respond to the circumstances that present themselves to us. And, unlike nonhuman animals, we must take responsibility for our decisions.

Obviously, we have not been able to control the circumstances that have confronted us, but we want to shoulder our responsibility for the future. We want to warn of the dangers of the animal rights movement by exposing some of its "dirty little secrets." At the same time, rather than hiding animal research itself as a "dirty little secret," we want to tell the story of medical progress that has come about through intelligence gathered from the humane use of laboratory animals.

A note on references: we want you, our readers, to be able to consult our sources and check on our use of citations. Text references direct you to a list of sources at the end of the book. When there is more than one listing for a source, a bracketed date in the reference identifies the one intended. Other numbers in the reference identify page numbers.

A GUIDE TO WORDS

As Lewis Carroll admonished, "We should say what we mean" when we use certain words. Here is what we mean by the following terms:

Animal research is discovery science, an enterprise of exploration into the unknown. When scientists seek to know something about the molecular or cellular or physiological workings of animals—and that includes us humans—they can, as part of their search, examine those workings first in nonhuman species, following up clues found in animals with studies of humans. Animal research is called biomedical research because it studies life (*bios*) for medical purposes. It is a basic science (see following) even though its questions are motivated by the desire to advance medical knowledge.

Animal testing, which is required by the Food and Drug Administration, involves one thing that is known—a drug or a therapy—and two things that are unknown—the efficacy and the safety of the drug or therapy. The idea for the known factor comes from basic research; the method for testing it involves, in the first instance, animals. After having obtained successful test results in animals and before securing approval for human use, researchers test drugs and treatments on humans.

* * *

Basic research is human questioning, trained and guided by scientific method, exploring the universe around us. Basic biomedical research is driven by the desire to understand and the hope that what is understood will contribute to the improvement of human and animal health.

Applied research brings knowledge gained in basic research to bear on the solution of specific problems. Once one group of basic scientists discovers the way in which certain hormones regulate the functioning of an organ, for example, they or another group can devise and test a drug or treatment that will correct the malfunctioning of that organ.

* * *

Private, when used of research, indicates that the funding making it possible comes from for-profit pharmaceutical companies—usually they test a drug or treatment—or from not-for-profit foundations such as the March of Dimes or the Howard Hughes Medical Research Institute, both of which also support basic research.

Public, when used of research, means that the funding making it possible comes from a federal agency, usually from the National Institutes of Health or the National Science Foundation. Such funding primarily underwrites basic research.

It is necessary because the for-profit sector cannot afford to wait thirty or forty years for discoveries to be applied in a profit-making way.

* * *

Animal welfare refers to the idea that humans have a responsibility to care for animals and to behavior and practices that seek their well-being or welfare. Because seeking animal welfare is in line with what is noblest in our human nature, it is sometimes called "acting humanely."

Animal rights designates the belief that animals, like humans, possess at least some inalienable rights. Often, though not in this book, animal rights is used as shorthand for any concern for animals, whether it be showing kindness to pets or promoting the belief that animals shouldn't be kept as pets.

Animal protection can mean most any idea or program, from animal welfare to animal rights, that is seen by its proponents as benefiting animals. Sometimes it is used in a more narrow sense for programs that benefit wild animals, especially endangered species.

Animal liberation is a term preferred by philosopher Peter Singer, who doesn't think that there are such realities as "rights," either for humans or for animals. He prefers to speak about the interests of animals, especially the interest they have, in his view, of living their lives in freedom, or liberation from human use.

* * *

Animal extremism is any attempt to change public policy as well as individual practice by such actions as mailing anonymous threats and envelopes armed with razor blades; posting on the Internet the names, addresses, phone numbers, and vicious characterizations of animal users; following those persons or their family members as they go shopping or to school; vandalizing their property; setting fire to the institutions and destroying equipment where they work; and, in the most serious cases, placing bombs beneath their cars or at their house doors.

* * *

Animal activism is any attempt to change public policy as well as individual thinking and practice by persuading legislators, educators, and all those who use animals by writing, conducting workshops, leafleting, debating, writing letters, organizing and lobbying, and performing acts of nonviolent civil disobedience. Except for the latter, these methods are legal, and in the case of the latter, activists are willing to accept arrest and punishment in order to draw our attention to a "higher law."

* * *

An *animal researcher* is one who practices animal research or animal testing.

Vivisector is a term of opprobrium for an animal researcher, carrying a sinister and cold connotation—the researcher cuts up living things ("vivi-sects") without justification or compassion.

* * *

Animal knowing or *elementary knowing*, shared by animals and humans, sizes up a taken-for-granted world, the world that is spontaneously or unthinkingly expected to be "out there." It involves dependable associations of "here" and "there," and "before" and "after," that allow all animals, humans included, to win sustenance and stave off predators.

Full-human knowing involves the irrepressible drive to understand the world we perceive around us. Our human questioning leads to insights into perceptions, judgments about the truth or adequacy of the insights, and decisions about "what in the world" we ought to do.

* * *

Conscious subjects is a description of most animals and human beings. Conscious subjects are aware of themselves and know the world around them. Because current law doesn't recognize any category other than things and persons, it treats nonhuman conscious subjects as things. We believe that animals are conscious subjects, but we do not believe that their consciousness entails the rights that belong to human beings. Persons are conscious subjects whose wonder about the world around them causes them to seek understanding, take responsibility for the truth of their insights, and give responsible direction to their lives. They hold themselves and others accountable for their actions. Personhood, which is recognized in law for all members of the human race, even infants, impaired and senile human beings, is the basis for rights.

* * *

A *pet* is an animal, usually domesticated, that is kept in the custody of and cared for by a person (*pet owner*) who has captured and tamed or, in all but a few instances, paid for the animal.

The terms *companion animal* and *animal guardian* denote the same as "pet" and "pet owner," but they suggest a reciprocal relationship in which the animal renders some service—companionship, seeing for the sightless, protection for the vulnerable—and the person provides food, shelter, and attention. Animal activists frequently introduce these terms into ordinances and statutes in order to advance the notion that animals have the rights not accorded to things that are owned.

* * *

Speciesism is a word coined by animal liberation philosopher Peter Singer for any idea or practice that treats members of one group differently than members of another group for no reason except membership in the group. Speciesism puts the interests of our human species above those of others simply because those species aren't human.

"Natural" speciesism is the speciesism that animal rightists believe to be wrong when practiced by human animals but acceptable when revealed in nonhuman animal behavior.

* * *

Ecology is the study of the relations between organisms and their environment.

Deep ecology is the belief that individuals and species are functional parts of the larger super-organism that is nature. Humans, in this view, exist wholly within rather than in any way above nature.

Stewardship is the notion that humans, in addition to playing various roles within the natural environment, have responsibility for nature, its healthy operation and its evolution.

* * *

Vegetarians eat no meat. Some people are vegetarians because of health reasons, others for the sake of the environment and economy—raising beef cattle, they claim, is a very inefficient use of the world's resources—and animal rightists because they believe that animals have the right not to be harmed or killed.

Vegans eat and use nothing that comes from an animal. That would include dairy products, wool, silk, and honey. Many vegans are animal rightists who avoid participating in any exploitation whatsoever of animals.

CHAPTER 1

IN THE CROSSHAIRS

"Excuse me," I said, cutting to the front of the line of passengers at the departure gate counter, "I have an emergency and need you to call the police right now!" Two airline agents stopped checking seating charts and looked at me with that look people give you when they are trying to figure out if you are serious, joking, or just plain nuts.

"The people behind me have been following and threatening me; please call the police." I was trying to be firm, but realizing just how paranoid I sounded, I added, "I am a medical researcher and they are protesting my visit to Tampa. They're not passengers (this was shortly before 9/11, when security measures allowed nonpassengers into boarding areas)," I continued, hoping to gain a bit of credibility.

"May I see your boarding pass?" one of the agents responded. I handed it over, certain that she was profiling me as delusional. She examined the pass, and then looked at my pursuers. I didn't turn around.

"OK, sir, we are going to board you right now," came the decision. She had believed me! Now she was whispering to the other agent, who began dialing the phone. In a few seconds, I was ushered on to an empty plane. I was sweating and could feel my heart pounding.

Some ten minutes later, the pilot boarded, walked back and asked if I was OK. I told him that I was happy, even surprised, that the agents had taken me seriously. He interrupted, "Didn't you see your name on their T-shirts: KEEP PRIMATE TESTER DR. P. M. CONN OUT OF U.S.F.?" In my anxiety, I had missed the detail that had made my story credible to the agents. I could feel my blood pressure returning to normal as the rest of the passengers began arriving on board.

I was en route to Tampa where I had been selected as a final candidate for the position of vice president for research at the University of South Florida. A few months later, I recounted the entire experience in public testimony in Portland, Oregon, during a hearing of the FBI's Joint Terrorism Task Force.

> My name is Dr. Michael Conn. I work as Special Assistant to the President of Oregon Health and Science University and as Associate Director of one of its institutes, the Oregon National Primate Research Center. I also have a research program that has contributed to the development of treatments for breast and prostate cancer, endometriosis, and problems of infertility.
>
> My own research program doesn't currently use animals, although it has in the past. Like most Americans, I understand the value of animal research in basic science that is so important for development of treatments for both human and animal disease. Therapies for diabetes, AIDS, Alzheimer's, cancer, along with antibiotics, vaccines, and surgical techniques—to name just a few things—all had origins in animal research. I have spoken and written about the importance of humane animal research and how it benefits humans and animals.
>
> Shortly before a recent trip, I was alerted that a Midwest activist had announced my visit to the University of South Florida on an animal rights Listserv. I later learned that this person believes that "we must be willing to do whatever it takes to gain animals freedom." When asked if this included killing "animal abusers," he reportedly had said, "I would unequivocally support that, too" (Lessenberry). This man, who had been paid for advertising work by People for the Ethical Treatment of Animals (PeTA), one of the world's largest animal rights organizations, urged subscribers to write letters to the university administration and to my academic colleagues. Some of the letters came to me, including an email from the educational coordinator of another animal rights

organization detailing my "ignominy" and telling me that I was unwelcome in Tampa, home of the university.

My plane was met by animal extremists who tried to engage and film me. Exercising their rights under a state open meetings law, they were present at most all of my scheduled meetings with university committees. Some stood outside meeting room doors to lobby attendees and distribute fliers that made outlandish claims. Others, wearing T-shirts that said "KEEP PRIMATE TESTER DR. P. M. CONN OUT OF U.S.F.," made derogatory comments. Still others asked me why I use primates, prompting a faculty sympathizer to accuse me of being a "son of a bitch" who was lying when I reported that I don't use animals in my current research program.

In one meeting, media burst into the room. They never interviewed me, but chose to accept unchallenged the claims made by the extremists and to identify me with a term of opprobrium used by extremists—"vivisector."

The campus was papered with handbills, full of absurdly incorrect information. Those responsible for the campaign of misinformation allowed no forum for dialogue, and one of them rebuffed my invitation to meaningful discussion. I received threatening calls at the hotel and knocks on the door in the middle of the night. All this justified the university's precaution in having an armed police officer assigned to look after me.

At the end of the first day, after being accused of telling lies and cursed at, all the while trying to address the academic concerns and questions of my colleagues, I considered returning home to Portland for my safety. Though my nerves were shot, I decided to remain in this stressful situation for the planned two days.

More was to come. To throw off harassers on the day of my departure, the police guard met me four hours before flight time in the lobby of the hotel, escorted me to a taxi, and followed me for a few miles before waving goodbye and turning off. With a tremendous sense of relief I checked in and headed to security. Suddenly, as I was about to step onto an escalator, I heard people muttering, "We came to say goodbye," and "We were afraid we missed you." I became aware that they had surrounded me. I managed to step outside their circle and descend the escalator several steps behind them. When I reached the gate, I was able to get an agent to phone airport police and get myself boarded onto the waiting but empty plane.

It still wasn't over. A couple of days later animal extremists shouted at me from the road above my home, and I found that someone had been ransacking my garbage.

Next, PeTA created a page to disparage me on its Web site and recruit correspondents to harass me with emails and letters. The site focused not on my own scientific investigations, but on the fact that I work for an institution that conducts animal research. It never mentioned, however, that my institution is fully accredited and in compliance with all federal and state laws.

When I was ten, twenty, thirty, or even forty years old, I would never have predicted that I would find myself, at age fifty, a target of the animal rights community. Yes, I have been interested in the biological process of life as long as I can remember. By the time I was twelve, I understood that cures for diseases required understanding how the body works when it is healthy. Even before that, I was a biology geek, crawling around on the ground to watch ants and growing seeds under different colors of plastic film.

I never trained to go into primate research and, frankly, knew little about monkeys, or "nonhuman primates" as I have learned to call them, until I arrived in Oregon in 1993. I spent the first part of my career at Duke University, working on rat-derived cell cultures. We used white rats and a handful of mice, all of them raised for the laboratory. We caused them no pain and killed them humanely to study their tissues.

Six years later, when I became a department head at the University of Iowa College of Medicine, I made the transition to continuous cell culture lines. Once growing and properly maintained, cell cultures divide and can be used for an indefinite period of time. This approach doesn't tell you much about the interactions of cells and organs in a whole animal, of course, but it is useful if you, like a watch repairman, want to understand the parts of a complex mechanism.

That's what I was, a kind of a biological watch repairman. By putting individual molecules together piece-by-piece I could learn how cells function. I knew that others, closer to the actual development of drugs, worked on whole animals. I knew, too, that the federal regulations and international law required that efficacy and safety tests be performed in animals before humans. I took comfort in that whenever I had to take a pill.

I had read a little bit about animal rights activities when I was in high school in the late 1960s. These activities were not front-page news. Mostly they were grumblings from "anti-vivisection" groups in the UK, distant and abstract. I heard of nothing happening in the United States. Activism when I went to college at the University of Michigan was directed to ending the Vietnam War. I watched protests with sympathy, struggling to maintain objectivity as I earned my way through the university reporting for radio stations on the antiwar movement. I watched people of conscience, including a roommate, get arrested for demonstrating their views.

I moved to North Carolina State University for an MS degree and focused my attention on hormone action. This interest continued as I went on to pursue a PhD at Baylor College of Medicine at the Texas Medical Center and then to a fellowship position at the National Institutes of Health (NIH). I was interested in how cells respond to the hormone GnRH and how GnRH might be used as a drug for the treatment of human and animal cancers and disorders of reproduction. I served as a consultant to drug companies and designed assays, or measurement methods that could be used to monitor the status of GnRH analogs in human serum samples. These same assays aided the studies of a number of colleagues who were working on animal models of human diseases. Sometimes they used monkeys, sometimes rats or mice, depending on the study.

Currently, as I mentioned in my testimony before the Portland City Council, I do not routinely use living laboratory animals of any sort. But, as Associate Director of the ONPRC, one of eight federally sponsored primate research centers, I work for a fully accredited institution that is responsible for the care of over 3,500 monkeys. This is a serious responsibility that involves frequent unannounced inspection visits by

the United States Department of Agriculture (USDA). We
support our animals with a veterinary and animal care staff of
ninety persons and a separate psychological enrichment program that includes seven more people led by a doctoral level
researcher. We also participate in a voluntary inspection program by an international professional organization, the Association for the Assessment and Accreditation of Laboratory
Animal Care (AAALAC).

Several things surprised me about my trip to the East Coast.
First was the fact that the communication among animal
extremists is so fast and effective. Although numbering only
fifteen at the most, a group of poorly informed and inarticulate
people was able to stir up fear on the search committee, a committee that had been highly supportive of me at first.

Second, I was shocked by the accusations. These people
charged me with "crimes" that I had never committed:
obtaining huge quantities of monkey sperm by a process that
they likened to genital electrocution, and torturing marmosets. When I tried to tell them I didn't use sperm and my
studies were all done in cell cultures, they shouted me down.

The truth that I wasn't allowed to explain was that some
investigators at our center and elsewhere routinely collect
monkey sperm by a process called electro-ejaculation. The
USDA and the veterinary community approve this process.
Despite its unfortunate name, the process isn't painful. A similar process is used for human paraplegics, otherwise unable to
father children.

What about "torturing marmosets"? Marmosets, I subsequently learned from the Internet, are very small monkeys.
Only recently, I noted the word "marmoset" on a paper listed
in my *curriculum vitae*. Of course! Sixteen years ago, I col-
laborated with a British colleague in measuring hormone lev-
els in some marmosets. For that contribution my name had
been added to the scientific publication's author list. I had
never seen the animals, the serum was shipped to me on dry
ice from England, and the animals were never harmed. They
had been injected with a harmless drug, and blood samples
had been taken. So *that* was the torture. My accusers had

created a "story-to-go" with a word they had read but, evidently, not understood.

The accusations lacked any basis in fact, and people who should have known better—the search committee, for example—accepted them as truth and acted on them. Hard to believe, but that is how animal rights groups do it. P*e*TA promoted the false accusations on its Web site: "Currently, Conn conducts painful, unscientific, and unethical gland research in marmoset, rhesus, and macaque monkeys." Huh?

Third, the president of the university, who had disclosed to me the ironic detail that she had grown up in a family of meat packers, and who had been personally gracious and supportive to me during the interview process, refused to speak with me further thereafter. After I returned home, I called and emailed her only to try to identify a strategy that would allow me to back out of the search process with a plausible excuse—"my wife prefers to live on the West Coast," for example—so that the animal rightists would not claim credit. In her return email, she ignored this concern, and she declined to return subsequent phone calls. The extremists, of course, did take credit for a victory.

The university eventually filled the position with an animal researcher, but one who wasn't in the crosshairs. His *curriculum vitae* referred to work on the hypertensive *rat* model, while his profile in the new job circumspectly omitted mention of his ongoing animal work and its potential for treating diabetes, stroke, and lung disease.

A final and most surprising twist: shortly after I presented my testimony in Portland, I received a certified letter from Jeffrey Kerr, a P*e*TA attorney, demanding that I immediately withdraw in a public forum my remarks about its payment to the Midwest activist who had alerted the university officials to my candidacy. (Kerr's call appeared quite curious some months later when the activist, Gary Yourofsky, officially went on the P*e*TA payroll. Later he was reportedly on a speaking retainer—$150 a crack. [Lessenberry])

One of my university's contract attorneys sent Mr. Kerr a letter expressing the legal equivalent of "piss off." Kerr must have done just that, for I never heard from him again.

Over more than a decade I learned two important lessons. First is the fact that some animal rightists misrepresent animal research and do so with impunity. Apparently they believe that they serve a cause greater than the truth. "Heavenly deception" is what some cult groups in the late 1960s called it.

Second, institutions that don't respond to misrepresentations and half-truths, attempting to hide legitimate and humane research as if it were a dirty little secret, play directly into the hands of animal rightists and extremists.

Were my harassers terrorists? It's your call, but remember that their actions were designed to coerce me by the threat of violence. Of course, some animal extremists might say, "We don't use violence. We demonstrate and destroy property, but we never injure or kill persons." What are we to think of that?

Maybe we should ask four ONPRC scientists who received letters armed with razor blades set to cut the hand of the opener. Would they think of that as violence?

Maybe we should ask ONPRC administrators, who receive anonymous telephone calls, unsigned mail, and emails from hard-to-trace Hotmail and Yahoo! accounts, expressing the wish that Primate Center scientists soon suffer in hell. Even if these communications stop prudently short of being illegal death threats, do the scientists feel the force of violence?

Or maybe we should ask the scientist at another university who has been warned that his children's pictures would be put up on the Internet—they would be made hostages, in other words—until he stops research on animals. Surely he experiences this as a violent threat.

The leaders of the animal extremist movement say that they are nonviolent in the tradition of Gandhi. They point out that unlike some of their colleagues in England, who recently took a baseball bat to the head of a researcher, they haven't physically assaulted or killed anyone. Perhaps not yet, but does that qualify them as nonviolent or put them in the league of Gandhi? Gandhi appealed to the consciences of British authorities, while extremists, bullying and intimidating, play to fear. Gandhi chose to endure suffering, while extremists set out to inflict suffering on others. Gandhi embraced *Satyagraha*, a relentless search for truth, while extremists post half-truths, at best, on their Web sites. Gandhi allowed himself to be arrested for his cause, while extremists phone anonymously and send unsigned emails.

One last note about what I learned on my journey to Florida. The only time during my stay there that extremists didn't follow me was when I visited the cancer ward at the University's hospital. Go figure.

CHAPTER 2

WAR STORIES

My trip to the East Coast in 2001 was a final lesson in my education about the animal rights movement and its war on animal research. That education had been proceeding apace ever since my move to the Northwest in 1993. Before then, I knew little about Portland and was unaware that it is an incubator for the movement. As I took up my position at ONPRC and Oregon Health and Science University (OHSU), I viewed the animal movement much as I had in high school—something distant and irrelevant.

On May 3, 1996, things started to change.

I arrived at work early in the morning to find two cars blocking the only entrance to our Primate Center. The drivers' necks were fastened with bicycle locks to the steering column of each car, and the keys to the cars and the locks were "lost." After firefighters sawed through the steering wheel, found the keys, "liberated" the drivers, and towed the cars, ONPRC officials signed complaints for second-degree criminal trespass against Craig Rosebraugh and three companions who identified themselves as members of the Liberation Collective.

Ineffective though it was, this event kindled my interest in the animal rights movement. I was working at a place where there were monkeys. These monkeys were well cared-for and received regular medical and dental attention. They were well fed and lived longer in our facility than did their relations in natural habitats. The Primate Center was approaching its fortieth year of uninterrupted compliance with federal regulations for their care. Nevertheless, we were being targeted by activists.

I began monitoring animal rights Web sites, following their Listservs, and gathering information from a handful of pro-research organizations, tiny operations operating on shoestring budgets that provided email summaries of animal rights activities.

One morning in October 1999, I received a startling post on one of the Listservs: a group calling itself the Justice Department posted a message saying it had sent razor blades to about eighty animal researchers. The blades had been fastened near the top of each envelope so that opening them by inserting a thumb under the flap would result in a severe cut. The blades, the letter announced, had been armed with rat poison. The enclosed letter called on scientists to abandon their research within twelve months, or "your violence will be turned back upon you."

I found four Primate Center investigators on the list of recipients. Being on the Pacific coast and an early riser, I was able to warn them, and we recovered all four envelopes unopened. These were transferred to law enforcement authorities, but to this day we have heard nothing about them. The twelve-month deadline to abandon research programs came and went without incident.

This action was intriguing, to say the least. The best-known animal rights organizations trumpet that they take steps to avoid harming humans or animals. Animal extremist groups like the Justice Department, which already in June 1994 had sent letter bombs to exporters of animals for food production (Justice Department), are not so careful. On the surface of things, there is a clean distinction of purpose and division of labor between animal rights and animal extremist organizations. It seemed, however, that underneath the surface there was a shadowy world of overlapping and interconnected memberships. The suspicion began to grow on us that extremists, who take credit for trashing labs and burning SUV dealerships at night, might disperse at dawn into larger organizations of animal rightists which, from behind the lines of their nonprofit 501(c)(3) boundaries, seldom condemn and often "understand" destruction of property and threats to life. Whether this is conscious strategy or "just the way things are," such overlapping would guarantee a flow of money from people who would be horrified to know what they are supporting.

CRAIG ROSEBRAUGH: IGNITING A REVOLUTION

So much for generalities; we return to Rosebraugh to see how porous is the line between activists and extremists and how rapid can be the evolution of an animal rights partisan to a revolutionary. In February 2002, one object of P*e*TA's financial largesse, the Earth Liberation Front (ELF), was attracting the attention of a congressional committee investigating domestic terrorism. Representative Scott McInnis called Rosebraugh to testify. At the time, Rosebraugh was running the ELF press office and serving as its spokesman. Members of the ELF and its sister group, the Animal Liberation Front (ALF), don't carry identification cards or have meetings. No one knows who all the members are. They could be four rebellious teenagers in upstate New York or a dozen zealots in Portland—it doesn't matter. What does matter is that these groups, after committing a destructive act—vandalizing a laboratory, burning new homes, harassing researchers, torching SUVs (Interview with ALF cell member)—need to take "credit" for the act lest its impact on the evening news is lost. Two unattributed and seemingly random fires on Long Island or in the Colorado Rockies have little significance; two "direct actions" by a national group brandishing a manifesto and a warning become the lead story. Operating a press office became the key strategy for "Elves" (as ELF members called themselves); through his press office Rosebraugh was able to get mainstream media to report the burning of buildings, a strategy that implicitly conveyed a threat to other property owners.

Point man Rosebraugh had developed a national reputation; "Sixty Minutes" featured him on a show in 2001 addressing efforts of the FBI to infiltrate the ELF (CBS [2] *60 Minutes*). Of course, as he told the media, he wasn't personally involved in destructive actions and had no idea who carried them out; he was only disseminating anonymous communications. He applauded and even promoted the actions, provided information on how not to get caught and on the legal consequences if you did (Donohue; Rosebraugh [2], 276). He became the titular leader of an invisible army. One could say that his troops hardly resembled the followers of Gandhi (Donohue).

It was clear that in the six years since he had been arrested outside the ONPRC, Rosebraugh had come a long way. As he described in his book, *The Logic of Political Violence: Lessons in Reform and Revolution* (Rosebraugh [2]), he was at the vanguard of a revolution that would gain rights for animals, end corporate oppression and liberate the Earth. Because Rosebraugh was in charge of the press office, the FBI, armed with search warrants, had seen fit on two occasions to search his home (Donohue).

On the first occasion, agents discovered a purple index card, duly reported in the local newspaper, containing my name and home address. Why this card was in his house, or what it might have portended, remains a mystery to this day. You can be assured that when I learned of the discovery, I felt not just the threat of violence, but something more, a violation of my person.

Rosebraugh, who earlier had spoken of his commitment to nonviolence, had shaved his head and taken to wearing Gandhi-like eyeglasses. He had obtained a Master's degree at Goddard College—an institution of higher learning that gives academic credit for life experiences and touts its role in taking students "to the forefront of the Environmental Wars"—with a thesis entitled, "Rethinking Nonviolence: Arguing for the Legitimacy of Armed Struggle" (ActivistCash [1]).

Requiring only a week of residence per semester, Goddard was a perfect fit for someone with obligations back in Portland, where Rosebraugh was running a vegan bakery. Rosebraugh's group launched a Web site with instructions for arson and bomb-making. He called it "Setting Fires with Electrical Timers: An Earth Liberation Front Guide" and produced a video called *Igniting the Revolution*, which urges people to burn homes and businesses in the cause of justice for all. When subpoenaed to testify before Congress in February 2002 as part of an eco-terror investigation led by Senator James Inhofe, Rosebraugh declined to respond to questions, just as he had the morning he attached himself to the steering column of the parked car in front of the Primate Center. In just a few years he had graduated from the misdemeanor of trespassing to near contempt of Congress. He avoided the latter, presumably on advice of counsel, only by providing written testimony.

I was especially interested in his responses to these questions, precipitated by an article in the paper noting that materials with my name had been found during a raid:

17) Do you know who Michael Conn is?
Michael Conn is a researcher at the ONPRC in Beaverton (OR). Conn wastes hundreds of thousands of federal tax dollars torturing and killing monkeys, a practice which has in no way benefited human health. . . .

19) Why was there an index card with Mr. Conn's name and home address in your residence? Was either ELF or ALF planning to take "direct action" against Mr. Conn or his property? If not, why was Mr. Conn's name and address in your possession?
See all objections, rights, and privileges asserted. . . .

50) Who first contacted you about serving as the spokesperson for the Earth Liberation Front? How did he/she contact you?
a) Jesus Christ
b) It was a spiritual sort of thing. . . .

51) During the time you served as spokesperson for the Earth Liberation Front, how did you support yourself?
Muffins. (Rosebraugh [1])

In all, Rosebraugh took the Fifth Amendment more than fifty times.

In her 1997 *Willamette Week* cover story on Rosebraugh, Elizabeth Manning recounted his efforts with the Liberation Collective to "stop all oppression" and, along the way, to "end all biomedical research" (Manning). She noted that at that time Rosebraugh was focusing on a Portland biomedical research institution (not mine) that killed *one* cat annually—in a state in which forty-six thousand cats were euthanized annually in shelters. Manning captured the absurdity of the situation in her article's title, "Saving The World, One Cat at a Time."

At one point, Rosebraugh professed to be proudly vegan, a lifestyle that excludes any animal-derived products (including honey, a product produced through the exploitation of bees). Veganism left him, in the words of *Willamette Week* writer Phil Dawdy, "whippet thin," carrying just 140 pounds on a six-foot, three-inch frame (Dawdy [2]). More recently, while advertising plans to open a vegan restaurant, Rosebraugh let slip that "due to a health problem, he's not currently a vegan, although he does stick to a vegetarian lifestyle in his diet and in his dress, which features black vegetarian shoes" (Donohue). We have no knowledge of the precise nature of his health condition, which included "dangerously low cholesterol," but chances are nine in ten that the medical diagnosis and any treatments for the condition depended, immediately or remotely, on animal research.

By the fall of 2003, Rosebraugh appeared to embrace the capitalism that he had previously sought to destroy in his *Ignite the Revolution* video: he announced the opening of the Calendula Café. According to its Web site, Calendula Café could be found in the "historic William and Elizabeth Jones House (circa 1891) [and] combines the rich elegance of a turn-of-the-century Queen Anne Victorian [*sic*] home with the modernity of a healthy and sustainable vegan menu." The beautifully restored building is located in Portland's hip Hawthorne district. A news story claimed that the $650,000 needed to open the café came from Rosebraugh's parents (Donohue).

If the menu was "sustainable," the business plan was not. Beset by a strike, an accusation of violating federal labor laws, and some attendant adverse publicity, the restaurant closed for several months in 2004. It reopened briefly, and then closed for good in October 2005. Rosebraugh at age thirty-three must have felt like any other failed restaurateur. According to one article (Donohue) he blamed the failure not on himself, but on those "rich, white men" in power.

In 2001, the North American Earth Liberation Front (ELF) was the recipient of a $1,500 contribution from P*e*TA. Further, according to a March 14, 2002, letter from P*e*TA's lawyer Jeffrey Kerr to Representative Scott McInnis, R-CO and chairman of the House Forest and Forest Health Subcommittee, this donation was "to assist [former ELF/ALF spokesman Rosebraugh] with legal expenses related to free-speech activities regarding animal protection issues" (Sokolowski).

You will remember Kerr, of course, as the very same attorney who had warned me against associating P*e*TA with terrorist groups. Six months before Kerr's letter to McInnis, when I spoke to the local city council in support of the Joint Terrorism Task Force's work protecting me and other researchers from extremists, even I would have been surprised by the revelation of an actual cash flow from P*e*TA to ELF.

A declassified document reports that already in 2001 FBI investigations had uncovered evidence confirming that there were connections between the extremist and rightist elements in the animal liberation movement (FBI). Information about the donation from P*e*TA to ELF appeared on a tax form that P*e*TA submitted to the IRS in 2000. The form specified that the purpose of the gift was "to support program activities" (Sokolowski). Reporter Jodi Sokolowski details some rather contorted attempts of P*e*TA to explain the gift. At first, P*e*TA director Ingrid Newkirk didn't remember the check. Then, a week later, she claimed it was for educational materials. The next day, she said on TV that it was being used for habitat protection. The explanations continued two days later when P*e*TA's director of policy and communications, Lisa Lange, declared that the money was for a program about vegetarianism. On March 14, P*e*TA lawyer Kerr wrote to Rep. McInnis that the $1,500 was "to assist [former ELF spokesman Craig] Rosebraugh with legal expenses related to free-speech activities regarding animal protection issues." Finally, Newkirk offered that the money assisted Rosebraugh for legal defense when he was subpoenaed to testify before McInnis's subcommittee (Sokolowski).

Rosebraugh has somehow developed an immunity from prosecution. The police haven't been able to touch him. Neither of two FBI raids of his living quarters ended in prosecution. His arrest at a demonstration in support of Mumia Abu-Jamal, a radical journalist imprisoned for murder, resulted in a $47,500 settlement from the City of Portland for the use of excessive force by the arresting officers, who caused his arm to be broken (Dawdy [2]).

In 2003, Rosebraugh gave an interview to a small anarchist magazine, *The "A" Word*. Here he revealed that destructive acts committed by the ELF were merely "reformist" and not nearly radical enough. They targeted one or another institution on a single issue, whereas what was needed was to bring down the entire power structure that supports injustice on every issue. "Whether one is concerned with human rights, environmental protection, or even animal advocacy," he said, "none of these single-issue concerns can be thoroughly addressed by reformist pursuits. A revolutionary movement is needed in the United States to at minimum allow for an atmosphere where there is a possibility of justice for all of these single-issue concerns" (Kargymm).

Rosebraugh's candor has resulted in an occasional appearance on national news with burning buildings in the background footage. In October 2003, he announced and promoted his new, self-published manifesto, *The Logic of Political Violence*. The cover features an image of the New York Twin Towers conflagration. Instructions to his readers indicate that the image was carefully and purposefully chosen:

Attack the financial centers of the country. . . . This can be done in a variety of ways from massive property destruction, to online sabotage, to physical occupation of buildings.

[Stage] large scale urban rioting. With massive unrest. . . . the U.S. government will be forced to send U.S. troops into the domestic arena thereby taking resources and political focus away from the [Iraq] war.

[Use] any means necessary shut down the national [media] networks. . . .

Spread the battle to the individuals responsible for the war and destruction of life. . . . Hit them in their personal lives, visit their homes, and make them feel personally responsible for committing massive atrocities.

Strike hard and fast and retreat in anonymity. . . . DO NOT GET CAUGHT. Do not get sent to jail. Stay alert, keep active, and keep fighting. Remember, an action is only good if it will serve to severely disrupt the political system of the country, its economy, and the corporate interests that drive it. (Rosebraugh [2], 276)

In late April 2004, at about the same time that the four employees were organizing their strike at the Calendula Café, police responded to a call about a mysterious fire in one of the restaurant's dumpsters. They found a sign that read: "Rosebraugh is a scab." The revolution was ignited—remarkably close to Rosebraugh's own home.

MATT ROSSELL: FOX IN THE HENHOUSE

Rosebraugh's attack on animal research had taken him down the path from demonstrating and disrupting to advocating property destruction and revolution. For the past few years, he has been missing in action in the animal research war. As of last information, his colleague, Matt Rossell, can be found, still today, on the picket line.

Rossell is very good with people. *Willamette Week* described his choirboy look as one of "perpetual innocence" (Dawdy [1]). He is clean and well groomed, seems honest and appears to be the kind of person that you might like your daughter to marry. Impressions can be deceiving.

Rossell came to work at the Primate Center under false pretenses and then showed us how a video camera, along with a little staging, some creative cropping, and lots of misleading captions, can tell a false but powerful story. It is a story that never ceases to be told and retold on the Internet and in mass mailings, even though it has been debunked in its entirety by independent investigation.

Had your daughter attracted Rossell's attention at the time that Rossell came to work at the center, she would've had to displace one Leslie Hemstreet. In the mid-1990s, Hemstreet was the co-editor of the *Earth First! Journal*, a publication of the radical environmental group, Earth First!

Of course, we didn't know of Rossell's connection to Hemstreet when we hired him as an animal technician in 1998. Neither did we know, until it was reported eight years later, that Rossell was a college buddy to Kevin Tubbs, and that they had shown up together in 1993 in cow costumes at an Iowa Cattlemen's Association meeting, where they were arrested for disorderly conduct and trespassing after yelling, "Meat is murder" (Freeman). Tubbs had found his way to the cozy incubator of activism that is Oregon, working as the assistant manager of a Castle Superstore pornography outlet. Meanwhile, he was reportedly active in a cell of the Earth Liberation and Animal Liberation fronts (*Bend Weekly*).

In July 2006, Tubbs and one of his several cell cohorts pleaded guilty to charges of conspiracy to commit crimes of arson and vandalism carried out across a five-state region. In May 2007, U.S. District Judge Ann Aiken, after declaring that four of the nine fires Tubbs was involved in—a forest ranger station, a police substation, a dealership selling SUVs, and a tree farm—were acts of terrorism intended to influence the conduct of the government or retaliate for government acts, sentenced him to twelve years and seven months in federal prison. "Fear and intimidation can play no part in changing the hearts and minds of people in a democracy," Aiken told Tubbs (Barnard, J.).

Rosebraugh was subpoenaed to testify in the Tubbs case, while Rossell and Hemstreet offered to post a $550,000 bond for bail. When we first read this, we thought that Rossell, who claims to be paid subsistence wages and has no health insurance by his current employer, In Defense of Animals (IDA), must have some very good contacts. Later, we were drawn to a "Motion for Release Pending Sentencing" filed in the United States District Court on January 8, 2007 (Friedman). In this document Tubbs' attorney indicated that, among other assets totaling $560,000, the Portland home of Hemstreet and Rossell, with an equity value of $265,000, would be pledged as a guarantee to the court that Tubbs would not be a flight risk. We took this to mean that they were more than just poker buddies.

Rossell was well liked by his coworkers in the Primate Center's Division of Animal Care. They were shocked when he surfaced from his underground operation and couldn't believe his betrayal of their trust. It took them several days to accept what had happened and to write a collective letter, published in the *Oregonian*, noting that even though they had petitioned center management to take better care of its employees, "they had never accused the center of mistreatment of animals" (Marshall).

P*e*TA's Mary Beth Sweetland considers Rossell one of its three best undercover workers (Dawdy [1]). She is high on Rossell because, in February 1996, P*e*TA went after Boys Town, using Rossell videos as ammunition in an aggressive media campaign against experiments there. Activists handcuffed themselves to the furniture in the office of the hospital's director, and a P*e*TA member dressed as the devil climbed onto the hospital's roof with a sign that read "Satan Loves Boys Town Cat Experiments" (Carlson).

Rossell's subterfuge at the Primate Center was so effective that when the local chapter of the Animal Legal Defense Fund announced a press conference to expose allegations of a "whistleblower" about animal abuse, we had no hint of who the "whistleblower" might be. Even after we learned it was Rossell, we did not realize that he had been working at our facility as an informant. Once we had satisfied ourselves that there was no basis to his accusations, we began to wonder about his motivation. One of our employees thought to do what hadn't occurred to us: to get on Google.com, which had made its debut not too long before. There she found Rossell's name in an article in the *Washington Post* that had been posted, of all places, on an animal rights Web site:

> In the spring of 1995, [P*e*TA's Mary Beth] Sweetland sent [Michelle] Rokke to Omaha to get a job at Boys Town National Research Hospital. . . . Sweetland wanted Rokke to investigate a neurological study that Edward Walsh and his wife, JoAnn McGee, were performing on cats, an experiment funded by a grant from the National Institutes of Health.
>
> Rokke managed to get a job as a housekeeper in the hospital, but the work took her nowhere near the cat experiment. "I didn't have much access to the place where the animals were kept," she says. "Basically, I scrubbed toilets and vacuumed rugs."
>
> She scrubbed and vacuumed for seven frustrating months, hoping to transfer into the lab. She never did, but *another P*e*TA spy, Matt Rossell, landed a job as a security guard and began secretly videotaping kittens that had undergone neurological surgery in the experiment.* (Carlson, emphasis added)

At that point, we knew that we had been set up. Floodgates of information opened. It turned out that in addition to the Boys Town operation, Rossell had a history of undercover work at the Walker Brothers Circus and the Aeschleman Fur Company, where he reportedly participated in the anal electrocution of five hundred foxes (Dawdy [1]).

Understanding what had happened to us is one thing, but dealing with the public relations nightmare created by animal rights Web sites that began springing up, all featuring Rossell's video images, was another, far more demanding thing altogether. Once published, lies take on a life of their own, and still today, the false images are distributed and appear on Web sites.

Philip Dawdy profiled Rossell in *Willamette Week* as an ingénue. He suggested that Rossell had taken the Boys Town job only for the purpose of earning money to move to Oregon. Offended by what he saw there, he photographed, documented, and contacted P*e*TA, which offered to pay him twenty thousand dollars for the job (Dawdy [1]).

Rossell played the role of "offended innocent." He was so convincing that long after he left our center some co-workers had trouble believing that he had been a plant. Rossell maintained an email correspondence with some of our employees in which he stuck to his story of "just being a technician" who was shocked and offended by what he had seen. It didn't hurt that these correspondents had voted Rossell to be "Employee of the Quarter" at the end of 1999.

Rossell, we discovered, had misrepresented himself on his employment application, omitting mention of previous work experiences and of a college education that would have flagged him as over-qualified for an animal technician's position. We were convinced that he had come to the Primate Center, not to work, nor even to observe objectively, but to create "evidence" and make his case.

Rossell was a capable photographer and master film editor. He portrayed baby monkeys that were in fact playing with their food as living in filth. He got his photographic shots early in the morning before cleanup. He photographed frightened animals, huddling, in what looked like crowded enclosures. Some of the "evidence" that he brought forward was so carefully contrived that it took us several days to figure out how he did it.

Rossell was smooth. At Boys Town he was so slick that, even after the story hit the news, his employer, Guardsmark, which supplied contract guards to Boys Town, continued to provide him a positive reference, noting to us that he was a "good kid" and had been "terrific for us." When we called them after our incident they seemed unaware that there had even been a problem at Boys Town.

As soon as Rossell's press conference about ONPRC began, animal rights groups began circling around for the kill. Ray Greek, president of Americans for Medical Advancement—it's hard to tell how many besides Greek belong to this antiresearch group—rushed forward with his comments on the lack of value of animal models, notably monkeys, in studying health. Of course, Greek did not mention that Rossell had once worked for his wife, veterinarian Jean Greek. She had attested to his skills in animal care at the time of his application for employment at the Primate Center. Veterinarian Sheri Speede, DVM, at that time head of the local chapter of IDA, weighed in, indignantly discounting the value of "any research derived from the use of a stressed out primate" and claiming, wrongly, that "the public cannot see what they're paying for" (Avgerinos).

Another veterinarian Isis Johnson-Brown, DVM, who, as a former employee of the USDA, had inspected the center, confirmed some of Rossell's allegations. In her statement, however, she failed to mention that some months earlier she had resigned abruptly from the USDA for reasons that both she and the agency refuse to disclose.

Once we knew the truth about Rossell, we contacted Dr. Edward Walsh, the previous object of Rossell's creative work for P*e*TA. He provided us a statement documenting his experience:

> It is clear that at least one faction of [the animal rights] movement would rather deceive than debate, rather hide in the dark of the night than operate in the open court of human opinion. I know this to be true because I have been there. I have experienced their cruelty and dishonesty personally . . . [Rossell's] time in Omaha led to extraordinary suffering for my family, including the theft of a significant part of life as a five year-old in the case of our son.

Walsh's reference to his son was explained in the Canadian magazine, *Macleans*:

> Animal-rights groups harassed their family mercilessly. Their home and offices were picketed and they received hundreds of

phone calls and letters. One letter went so far as to send a death threat in the form of false condolences for their son, then five years old. "So sorry to hear about the tragic death of your son. At least now he's in God's good hands, with all the beautiful kittens from the living hell you both created at Boys Town. (Kim)

"The impact on our family is virtually impossible to assess," Walsh told the same magazine, "It's a life-altering experience to have your life, and the lives of your children, so exposed. Routine daily habits—like turning an ignition switch or walking across a parking lot—can become anxiety-ridden."

Note that Walsh, whose work at the Boys Town facility focused on congenital deafness, was cleared of all of the claims that Rossell had made. Investigators from the NIH and the USDA noted that his research animals were anesthetized during the procedures, felt no pain, and recovered without any permanent impairment from their surgery.

As he had done in the case of Boys Town, Rossell made a number of outrageous allegations about our facility. None of these were supported by extensive federal investigations that followed. Five investigators, all veterinarians, worked daily for two weeks but found no merit in Rossell's claims and found no signs of animal cruelty or federal noncompliance. Animal abuse would have been impossible to hide in this investigation or in the ten unannounced inspections that extended our continuous USDA certification to over forty years. The Primate Center and Walsh's research program were cleared of any wrongdoing.

The investigators have departed, but Rossell's images remain. We first discovered these images in the moments following the August 2000 press conference on an elaborate Web site paid for by the California office of IDA. The Web site featured video clips, still images, and pages of cleverly worded accusations.

One of the videos showed a "hungry and filthy" monkey in an incubator. In reality, the infant had been given human baby food and had, like human babies, played with it and smeared the puree on the incubator window. The video had been made at an opportune moment before daily cleanup. Make a movie of a human baby in a highchair, covered with banana mush, and claim child abuse!

From this same video clip came a still photo, frozen at the instant when the infant face reveals what looks like anguish. This was puzzling until we went back to the video and noticed a rubber-gloved finger moving over the window of the incubator and toward the monkey. In expectation of food, the monkey moves toward the finger, pursing its lips and producing, for less than a second, the look that Rossell reduced to a still. The monkey was not upset or in pain, just caught in an unflattering pose.

Rossell's words and pictures don't tell an accurate story. Other images presented animals living in what looks like crowded conditions and in the midst of feces covering the floor. These images had been carefully cropped to suggest crowding, and most of the "feces" were Purina Monkey chow biscuits photographed from a distance in the dim light of dawn before morning cleanup. The photographer, having entered their enclosure, had likely frightened the monkeys—a direct stare is a threat to monkeys and a camera must appear to them as a giant eye—and they had huddled in the normal macaque response to any invasion of their space.

Another clip showed a room of monkeys banging their cages. The interpreter explained that the monkeys were being driven crazy by their confinement. But, in this instance, Rossell's cropping wasn't careful enough. At the bottom right of the video image we can see the food cart, and any animal technician will tell you that monkeys bang their cages in excitement when they see food coming.

Still another video displayed an infant sucking its penis. The allegation was that this behavior, a symptom of anxiety and sadness similar to a human baby's sucking its thumb or toes, had been caused by confinement and isolation. We looked up the infant monkey's medical history and found that he had been living in an outdoor, one-acre corral. His mother had abandoned him. The animal care staff had brought him inside for medical attention and some tender care. That is when the video was made. A few months later, thanks to the alert professionalism of the caretakers, the little monkey was back to normal. Outraged correspondents told us that pictures don't lie. Of course they don't, but cameras do what photographers want, and photographers can intend to misrepresent. Our correspondents might well have cited another adage that a picture is worth a thousand words. The center launched an Internet site to explain the truth behind each of Rossell's images. We also reported on the USDA investigations and subsequent USDA and AAALAC inspections. All that we published was to little avail.

We might well change the adage: a picture is worth thousands of dollars. In 2002, Rossell and IDA sent out a fundraising letter that capitalized on the emotional impact of his misleading images. Then again, in late 2003, they sent out still another appeal, asking desperately for immediate contributions, and once again the images, lacking any acknowledgment that there had been a controversy about their making, did most of the begging. In 2005, IDA, where Rossell is now the Northwest co-coordinator, continued to use their contrived images as fundraisers.

Rossell's images may not represent reality, but they continue to poison the world in which we work and live.

RICK BOGLE: EVOLUTION OF AN ACTIVIST

In Rosebraugh's undertakings we observed the enlargement of a cause, from single-issue protests to large-scale revolution. Rick Bogle's endeavors reveal the personal evolution of an extremist.

I first spoke with Rick Bogle in 1999, during the weeks that he sat on a plastic lawn chair on the public sidewalk in front of our Primate Center. He was there, of course, to protest primate research. During this time he accepted donations of stuffed monkey toys from passersby that he added to what he called his "Ape Army." He seemed interested in discussion and even allowed me to photograph him.

After serving in the Peace Corps in Liberia, Bogle became a schoolteacher in Prairie City, Oregon. There he remained eight years, evidently earning respect from the rural community as he taught math to middle-schoolers. His troubles began when he announced classroom rules forbidding, for moral reasons, the killing of insects and spiders; they ended when he lost his teaching position after hosting a three-day animal rights symposium in the school building. It seems that his views were a bit too extreme for the ranching and hunting community in which he lived.

Bogle began a correspondence with ONPRC officials in 1997. His letters were alternately insulting and mocking. In one sent to the director, for example, he announced as a fact that she "disregards the suffering of animals." Then he pleaded, "Please understand, I am trying only to gain some empathy for your position." Words like "incarceration [of monkeys]," torment [of monkeys]," and "holocaust [in research]" flowed from his pen.

It was a belligerent correspondence, but we thought it harmless until September 2001, when he initiated a curious and seemingly random attack on Dora E. Angelaki, PhD, a faculty member at Washington University in St. Louis. Angelaki means "Little Angel," a name that Rick bestowed on her, with mocking irony, on a Web site he established in her honor. In one of his postings he wrote, "The Little Angel of St. Louis is a portrait of the full ascension to equality for one woman involved in the pursuit of knowledge for knowledge's sake. It has taken bravery and an unflinching callousness in the face of unspeakable suffering" (Bogle [1]).

Unspeakable suffering? What Bogle didn't explain are the steps taken by Dr. Angelaki to eliminate pain. She performed her procedures on living animals only when the animals were in deep anesthesia. Bogle referred to her experiments as "bizarre," suggesting that only he has the framework to understand them. He never mentioned the extensive scientific

review that occurred to get the studies funded or the obliga-
tory animal protection review that occurred at the institution.
Bogle went on to summarize her career and reference her
publications, while interjecting comments demeaning the
value of her work and suggesting, inaccurately, that she tor-
tures animals (Bogle [1]). He did not, or perhaps chose not,
to understand that Angelaki's work has taught us how we ori-
ent ourselves in three-dimensional space. It tells us how the
body distinguishes gravity from movements of the head—
information critical for space exploration and for the effective-
ness of airplane pilots and underwater divers.

Any trace of reasonable dialogue disappeared in October
2003, when Bogle posted the following on a primate Listserv,
following the accidental death of a California animal
researcher in a car accident: "Though it cannot be argued that
the death of any vivisector is anything but a net good, Russel
L. De Valois' death and his wife's injuries would have been
more meaningful if the tire had failed as the result of some
thoughtful tampering" (Bogle [2]). Only weeks earlier, he
had also sent to a large number of animal researchers a message that said, among other things,

> Greetings Slime:
>   No clearer example of evil incarnate exists than the informed
> decision to use other primates in hurtful experimentation.
>   Your elimination is justified. You are a cancer. You are a
> blight on the progress of humane ethics and compassion, a pox
> on our moral and ethical progress. (Bogle [3])

Police and others felt this was threatening. In 2006, Bogle
excused this message as something written while drinking
alcohol (Rivedal). When called by the university security
office, he insisted that violence was not his intent. When contacted by OHSU's Public Safety Office, however, he suggested otherwise and appeared to defend his stance:

> The message I sent, and will be sending to many other people
> engaged in similar studies was wholly appropriate.

The claim that the message was "threatening" is certainly true. These people's livelihood, their free access to more victims is definitely threatened, as is their continuing rich economic rewards. Any further threat they might feel after being told that at least one person finds them to be among society's most distasteful scum is simply their guilt-driven projection. (Bogle [4])

The "Little Angel" site was taken down in early October 2003, shortly after Bogle's comments and emails to investigators. He had taken up residence in Madison, Wisconsin, to turn his venom on the Primate Center there. Always a bit quixotic, the general of the Ape Army is attempting to establish a museum that will exhibit the "horrors" of animal research at the Wisconsin Center.

Kevin Kjonaas: What the Future Holds

It is one thing for an activist to send vituperative and threatening letters to scientists, effective as they might be in occasioning second thoughts about careers and creating a climate of research fear. It is another thing, an endeavor much vaster and more ominous, for a (subsequently convicted) activist to direct a campaign of harassment to bring an institution to its knees. Such is the mission of Kevin Kjonaas. His campaign to shut down Huntingdon Life Sciences (HLS) portends things to come for universities and research institutions.

As I am writing this in 2006, Kjonaas, born Kevin Jonas, has passed through his mid-twenties. He explains that he uses the "Kjonaas" alias to spare family members from harassing phone calls from people who oppose the tactics and aims of his group, Stop Animal Cruelty-USA (SHAC-USA). It is hard to locate Kjonaas's phone or address on the Web sites that he allows to use his names. His precautions are ironic; the SHAC-USA organization he heads specializes in telephone, fax, and email harassment.

Kjonaas entered adulthood as a University of Minnesota political science student and former director of that institution's

Student Organization for Animal Rights. In the days following a 1999 University of Minnesota laboratory break-in, he was widely quoted as an ALF spokesman, although he denied any personal knowledge of the break-in. "The ALF chose to use direct action when other activities had failed," he told *New Scientist* magazine (Kleiner). Walter Low, whose lab at the university was vandalized, says that cell cultures were destroyed (Kaiser). The irony is rich: animal rightists argue that researchers should be using cultures instead of animals—precisely what Low was doing.

Since then, Kjonaas has become national director and spokesperson for SHAC-USA and perhaps the first to applaud terrorism:

Today's terrorist is tomorrow's freedom fighter. (Canada Free Press)

Why should any one of us feel that "it shouldn't be me taking that brick and chucking it through that window?" [or think] "Why shouldn't I be going to that fur farm down the road and opening up those cages?" It's not hard; it doesn't take a rocket scientist. You don't need a 4-year degree to call in a bomb hoax. These are easy things, and they're things that save animals.

And so I want all of you in this room to, A) Question not just what is right and wrong, but what is effective, and B) why can't all of us be doing it?

I think the animal rights movement is strong—that's my opinion. [But] it's time to start flexing our muscles. (O'Connor)

According to its critics, the main goal of SHAC-USA is to put HLS out of business. "Closing HLS is my life and this campaign will remain my life until HLS is closed," Kjonaas reportedly informed us (Carnell [1]). Much of the information on HLS that he has posted has come from Michele Rokke, whom we have met already as a colleague of Matt Rossell and an undercover worker sent by P*e*TA to HLS between October 1996 and May 1997. It is reasonable to conclude that much of the basis of Kjonaas' determination comes from Rokke's stack of daily logs and videos (Green).

It is a fact that HLS has been cited for violations. Many of them were omissions in documentation. Some were more serious and resulted in two HLS employees being convicted of animal cruelty. None of the violations, however—not even the reprehensible cruelty of an employee who punched a beagle—warranted SHAC's terrorism.

Let's explain what it means to Kjonaas to target someone. It means jamming phones, faxes, and email systems (sometimes called "electronic civil disobedience"). It means bombarding computer servers so that they do not function (a so-called "denial of service" attack). It means making threats of physical violence, and it means including families in those threats by publishing such personal data as social security numbers and credit card information (Cook).

Should there be any doubt, SHAC's email to a Chicago insurance executive makes it clear that the organization is engaged in terrorism: "You have been targeted for a terrorist attack. If you bail out now, you, your business, and your family will be spared" (*Chicago Daily Herald*). And, should there be any doubt about how SHAC attacks are perceived, consider this from HLS regulatory affairs officer Jim Baxter: "Everything that comes through the door I open at arms length, using a long-bladed letter opener. No one should have to fear his or her mail" (Baxter, 70–71). UK Trade Minister Alan Duncan, agrees, "It's animal terrorism" (ActivistCash [2]), and UK Home Office Minister Mike O'Brien notes, "These are thugs posing as protesters—a tiny group of activists succeeding where Karl Marx, the Baader-Meinhof gang, and the Red Brigades failed" (ActivistCash [2]).

In the course of SHAC's successes, the ever-gentle Ingrid Newkirk, President and Co-founder of P*e*TA, gloated, "More power to SHAC if they can get someone's attention" (*Boston Herald*). Consider what happened to Brian Cass, CEO of HLS, one night in February 2001 as he was getting out of his car at his home in England. Without any warning, three masked men beat him on the head and body with what some reports said were baseball bats and other reports ax handles. According to Detective Chief Inspector Tom Hobbs of the Cambridgeshire Police, "It's only by sheer luck that we are not beginning a murder inquiry (BBC [1]).

A later attack with a chemical spray got the attention of Cass' marketing director and left him temporarily blinded and writhing in pain. Two large chunks of cement crashing through the plate glass doors of their patio got the attention of two employees of a company doing business with HLS, as did a strange package delivered to their house and containing explosives to kill anyone who might have dared to open it. A dozen protesters shouting vulgarities day and night in front of his home got the attention of an American insurance salesman whose clients included HLS. And, in case his mind wandered, "Wanted for Murder" signs posted around his neighborhood, gallons of red paint poured on his doorstep on Fathers' Day, a re-routing of his mail to a post office box without his knowledge, and the posting on the Internet of his social security number, his and his wife's license plate numbers, and details of their daily routine helped bring him back to attention (ActivistCash [3]).

When a company doesn't comply with SHAC's demands, the next step is to target its lending institutions, stockholders, brokers, vendors, suppliers, and customers until the company is, quite literally, unable to do business. According to Brian Carnell, Kjonass promised, "We'll take out their customers [and] their workers" (Carnell [1]).

So it was that a year after these escapades already mentioned, a small band of extremists wearing ski masks barged into the Portland, Oregon, offices of Marsh, Inc., circled around employee desks, set off a noise maker, shouted allegations, and slapped animal rights posters on the walls. Afterwards, I had lunch with the head of the office, and he reported that startled workers had no idea what the ruckus was about, but that when they learned that a Marsh, Inc., office in another city insured HLS, some chose not to remain vulnerable to further harassment and terminated their employment (personal communication).

Stephens, Inc., extended a loan in 2003 to HLS, which is, in Kjonaas' words, "enemy number one in this country" (Americans for Medical Progress [1]). Kjonaas announced constant protests against Stephens, Inc., and its officials at their offices, on the golf course and in their homes until the company called in its loan to HLS. He noted that targeting companies through motions at shareholder meetings is not enough. It is more uncomfortable for investors and more effective for the campaign to target them at home and in their offices (*Huntingdon Life Sciences vs. Stop Huntingdon Animal Cruelty*).

The animal liberation magazine *Bite Back* published an open letter from unnamed SHAC supporters to an executive at Columbia Asset Management, a firm that SHAC says invests in HLS:

> We have "bumped into you" at Genuardi's and watched you in and out of [drug store] CVS—but I guess you didn't notice [*sic*]. We followed when you took your little brat to the Gymboree and then to Chuck E Cheese's. We know you take that little brat to the doctor at Buckingham Pediatrics, and we made sure that they were sent information about HLS and how you and your husband make money off of animal cruelty. (*Bite Back*)

Shaklee Corporation and Chiron, which were believed to have business relations with Huntingdon, were subjects of bomb attacks in September 2003 (Green). SHAC activists may have targeted Shaklee since its parent company, Yamanouchi Consumer Inc., hired Huntingdon to perform leg-breaking experiments on beagles about six years ago (Pristin). The studies were done—under anesthesia so that the animals felt no pain—in order to develop new approaches to bone mending. But a SHAC spokesperson decided that she spoke for all of us when she told an ABC affiliate in San Francisco: "The public became outraged at the idea of these beagles having their legs sawed to test an osteoporosis drug, and the beagles were freed from Huntingdon and placed into homes" (KGO).

Of course, Kjonaas says he doesn't know the fugitive charged with the bomb attacks (Taylor). He and his group just publish information about targets on their Web site. It remains to be seen in trial whether Kjonaas did or didn't know exactly who the vandals were—like terrorists, animal rights extremists work in independent cells unknown to each other. "That [publishing information about extremist hits] is within the confines of our first amendment rights in the United States," Kjonaas reportedly noted. "It may be controversial and you may not like it, but you can't stop us." Kjonaas was confident: "The FBI can't arrest us on anything, they can't indict us on anything" (Kjonaas).

Nevertheless, arrest Kjonaas the government did. In 2003, the FBI's Joint Terrorism Task Force entered and searched the U.S. East Coast offices of SHAC. Not long afterwards, the government issued a five-count federal indictment that charges each of the "SHAC 7" (Kevin Jonas—the documents revert to his legal name—Lauren Gazzola, Jacob Conroy, Darius Fullmer, John McGee, Andrew Stepanian, and Joshua Harper) with violations of the 1992 Animal Enterprise Protection Act, the first law that explicitly seeks to protect animal industries from animal rights vandalism (Carnell [2]).

As a bonus Jonas, Gazzola, and Conroy were also charged with conspiracy to stalk HLS-related employees across state lines, along with three counts of interstate stalking with the intent to induce fear of death or serious injury in their victims. Each of the charges brings a maximum $250,000 fine. The main charge of animal enterprise terrorism carries a maximum of three years in prison, while each of the charges of stalking or conspiracy to stalk brings a five-year maximum sentence (Carnell [2]).

Some law enforcement officials think it's just a matter of time until animal extremists assault or kill someone (Bai).

Meanwhile, should there be any doubt about whether SHAC attacks work, SHAC's Web site lists an "honor roll" of some fifty companies that have "dumped" HLS, including Charles Schwab, the world's largest online broker; Marsh, Inc.; Citibank; Merrill Lynch; HSBC; and Deloitte & Touche

(SHAC [1]). HLS corporate value has shrunk by over 90 percent, and its share price has plummeted so dramatically that
the firm has been delisted by the New York Stock Exchange.

In the fall of 2005, a company related to HLS, Life Sciences Research, Inc. (LSR), was scheduled to be listed on the
New York Stock Exchange. The champagne breakfast that is
customarily hosted by the NYSE for executives of companies
to be listed was in progress when a Stock Exchange official
entered the room to announce a last minute decision—LSR
would not be listed after all. Thomas Donlan of the financial
newspaper *Barron's*, notes that the "New York Stock
Exchange did not want to become Ground Zero for animal-
rights protests" (Liberty Watch).

Fourteen months later, the NYSE, acting only shortly
before the relative quiet associated with the Christmas holiday—the announcement came "after the bell" on the Friday
before Christmas Monday—declared that LSR would, indeed,
be listed on the NYSE Arca. NYSE Arca is the first U.S. all-
electronic stock exchange, one with electronic execution and
open, direct, and *anonymous* market access (Americans for
Medical Progress [2]).

This decision appeared to be related to a settlement agreement under which LSR released NYSE from all claims relating
to the September 2005 "postponement" of its listing.
SHAC's response came on January 8, 2007, when its Listserv
launched "Operation Fightback" and called on "groups
across the world to target the New York Stock Exchange"
(SHAC-UK). How that will be done remains to be seen.

On March 3, 2006, Conroy, Fullmer, Gazzola, Harper,
Kjonaas, and Stepanian were convicted of coordinating and
encouraging an onslaught of harassment and intimidation
against employees of HLS (U.S. Department of Justice [1]).
On September 12, 2006, the day following the fifth anniver-
sary of 9/11, the sentencing began. First, Federal District
Court Judge Anne E. Thompson sentenced the SHAC organization itself to a restitution order of one million and one dollars. Each of the defendants learned that they were to be held
personally responsible for this sum until the debt is paid off.

Additionally, the organization was given a mandatory fine of $2,400 ($400 for each of six criminal counts). Then, Kjonaas was sentenced to seventy-two months in prison. Gozzola, Conroy, Fullmer, and Harper received sentences of fifty-two, forty-eight, thirty-six, and twelve months, respectively. All defendants were given three years probation after release from prison and a mandatory $600 special assessment fine. Stepanian, although convicted only on a single count, received thirty-six months, in recognition of his significant criminal history.

Following the sentencing, each defendant was given an opportunity to speak. Kjonaas, in an uncharacteristically modest mood, seemed disoriented: "I'm utterly humbled. I came here with my mother. This has been a traumatic experience, a learning experience, and I don't know what more I could say." Judge Thompson, however, recalled the convicted man's mood on another occasion, a taped conversation in which "anyone who listened would recognize a sense of glee, almost, in wielding power" (Mansnerus).

As U.S. Attorney Christopher J. Christie noted on the day of the SHAC conviction, "The verdict reveals these individuals for what they really were: thugs who went far beyond protected speech and lawful protest to engage in and incite intimidation, harassment and violence" (U.S. Department of Justice [1]). Christie clearly took satisfaction in ending some of the activities of SHAC in the United States. His pleasure would have been ephemeral, however, had he monitored SHAC's British Listserv. On September 18, 2006, it introduced a new target, Hubnet Express; provided email addresses for employees and phone and fax numbers for offices of the company; and urged readers to make contact with them. All that was different was a disclaimer that nothing in the action alert has the purpose of inciting any form of harassment or illegal action (SHAK-UK).

A lot had happened. The American perpetrators of the actions against HLS had been sentenced, and the splashy graphics of the www.shacamerica.net Web site were reduced to one sentence, "We apologize, but this site has been shut down for legal reasons." You might think that while this was going on, HLS would have begun to feel some relief. Not so. The worldwide web is truly worldwide, meaning that legal actions in the United States have little impact on email and Internet activities from abroad. The pressure and threats continued. The stock, which had traded above eighteen dollars per share before the September 2005 date on which they were to join the NYSE, was trading at barely nine dollars in early May 2006 (BBC [5]).

Another animal extremist group, Win Animal Rights (WAR)—joined in the chorus of self-congratulation, touting its own contribution to HLS' demise through "Operation Knockout": "Columbia Management, investment subsidiary of Bank of America, has divested their shares in LSRI (aka Huntingdon Life Sciences or HLS). With this confirmed, Win Animal Rights (WAR) declares Operation: Knockout, launched on January 6, 2006, successfully completed on May 1, 2006" (Boston Animal Defense League). The message contained yet another threat about to be unveiled: "Now it is time to turn our attention to the customers and suppliers of HLS. Stay tuned for the launch of our next bold and exciting operation . . . coming soon." Other WAR emails claimed capitulation from major financial institutions and stock traders worldwide. Among these:

Market Makers ("traders"):
    Bear Stearns, Bernard Madoff, Cantor Fitzgerald, Chardan Capital Markets, Collins Stewart Tullett/Burlington Capital Markets, Dalton, Greiner, Hartman, Maher & Co, Jones Trading, Merriman Curhan Ford & Co, Legacy Trading, Neuberger Berman, Penson Financial, Sterne Agee, Seaboard Securities, Tradition Asiel Securities, Vertical Group.

Institutional Investors:
    Awad Assets, American Century Investments, Columbia/Bank of America, Cramer Rosenthal & McGlynn, Fidelity Investments, Washington Mutual.

If private businesses are so quick to cave in, what will happen when SHAC turns its full attention to public universities and publicly funded research facilities? Will those institutions choose to shed research programs that become targets and try to save the rest by hiding them in what becomes a "dirty little secret"? There is reason to hope that that won't be the case. Businesses have stockholders and a responsibility for the bottom line, but the research enterprise has stakeholders and responsibility to people who look for cures and treatments for the diseases that afflict us. Patients—and who will not be a patient at some time?—hold the key to the future of biomedical research.

CHAPTER 3

THE ANIMAL RIGHTS MOVEMENT PAST AND PRESENT

Shock and indignation were the reactions in 1975 when Peter Singer, until then a little-known philosopher, called for the liberation of all animals from human use in a widely popular little book, *Animal Liberation* (Singer [2]). His indictment of animal research seemed so obvious. Why, we might have asked, hadn't we thought before that

- animals and humans are so different that it is pointless to apply the results of animal experiments to humans;
- animal pain (as well as its relief through anesthesia) interferes with experimental results;
- alternatives to animal research are available;
- disease prevention through better hygiene is a surer way than animal research to improve public health;
- healing through observation, counseling, "natural" drugs, and homeopathy are more effective than scientific medicine;
- animal research, even if beneficial, is ethically unacceptable because it causes pain to living creatures;
- physical health and longevity are not the most important values in life. (French)

As a matter of fact, many people did think about all this—over a century ago. The above list of what seemed to be new and startling claims has been compiled from newspapers of the late 1800s, not the 1990s.

BACKGROUND: ENGLISH ANTIVIVISECTIONISM

Visits to England by two French scientists frame a half-century of British controversy about animal experimentation. François Magendie arrived in London in 1824 to lecture on his discoveries about the role of the spinal cord in sensory and motor control. By conducting surgeries on a puppy litter, Magendie had discovered and described the function of dorsal and ventral spinal nerve roots, an achievement that corrected opinions on the subject held by an English scientist, who had relied on "armchair" deductions from anatomical appearances. Yet, it had also been an achievement that involved undeniable suffering for the puppies. It was no surprise that Magendie's visit became an occasion for public demonstrations.

Just two years earlier, growing English sentiment for animal welfare had culminated in Parliament passing legislation, Martin's Act, to protect draft horses and domestic cattle from abuse. The Magendie uproar shifted the focus of popular concern for animals from their use in agriculture, entertainment, and sport to their use in physiological research. Physiologists had been making good progress in understanding the cells, tissues, and organs of living creatures, but until the late 1840s their advances depended on the use of unanesthetized animals. At least until 1847 and the discovery of anesthesia, there was plenty of reason for concern.

The other infamous French physiologist to visit England and stir up antivivisectionist sentiment was Eugene Magnan. In 1874, he appeared before members of the British Medical Association to demonstrate how to induce experimental epilepsy in a dog by injecting it with absinthe. Horrified observers interrupted the procedure, and a melee requiring police intervention ensued. Urged on by antivivisectionists, the Royal Society for the Prevention of Cruelty to Animals filed charges, accusing English doctors who were present of violating Martin's Act. The jury, on a technical finding that the prosecution had failed to prove that the named defendants had indeed participated in Magnan's procedure, voted to acquit, but physicians and physiologists in general stood condemned in the court of public opinion. In the years after 1876, the tide of antivivisectionism retreated. An important factor, of course, was the discovery of anesthesia. Since 1847 much physiological research had been conducted with animals under anesthesia. Just as important was the regulation of research mandated in the 1876 Cruelty to Animals Act. Its passage persuaded ordinary folks that physiological research would be conducted ever after in a responsible and, as far as possible, painless manner. One person who declared satisfaction with the new law was Doyle. Even though he consistently took the side of physiologists in letters to editors and in stories about Sherlock Holmes, he welcomed the law because of his memories of one of his instructors in medical school: "He was, I fear, a rather ruthless vivisector, and although I have always recognized that a minimum of painless vivisection is necessary, and far more justifiable than the eating of meat as a food, I am glad that the law was made more stringent so as to restrain such men as he" (Key, 192).

Ultimately, antivivisectionism failed simply because the public could not be convinced that the use of animals in advancing the knowledge and treatment of disease was immoral or futile. Surely, people did not want to see animals, especially pets, mistreated. For that reason they welcomed regulations on research. Nevertheless, once alerted by doctors of the British Medical Association that progress in treating disease depended on animal research, they became wary of the abolitionist agenda. They trusted physicians such as Doyle, who pleaded that "The interests at stake [in the antivivisection controversy] are so vital that an enormous responsibility rests with the men whose notion of progress is to revert to the condition of things which existed in the dark ages before the dawn of medical science" (Key, 195).

The arguments of physicians were buttressed by the accumulating successes of scientists. Researchers demonstrated beyond doubt that microscopic organisms are responsible for disease, and they laid the groundwork for medical treatments and public health measures that would remove one by one the threat of anthrax, cholera, rabies, diphtheria, and typhoid. The judgments of the movement's historian and of a contemporary animal rights theologian converge intriguingly. The historian, Richard French, observes that "On the simplest reading, the decline of antivivisection was in direct proportion to the success of the experimental approach," and the theologian, Rev. Andrew Linzey, comments ruefully that the movement lost its way when it committed itself to the untenable proposition that animal research cannot be scientifically necessary: "This line . . . that vivisection is useless . . . has cost the antivivisection movement dearly" (Linzey, 24).

DÉJÀ VU ALL OVER AGAIN?
THE ANIMAL RIGHTS MOVEMENT

The contemporary animal rights movement began with a scandal. In 1966, a *Life* magazine cover story documented deplorable living conditions at the facility of an animal dealer who supplied dogs to research institutions. Public indignation moved the U.S. Congress to respond swiftly. Its Animal Welfare Act, which translated humane principles into specific regulations governing the sale, treatment, and use of laboratory animals, became the law of the land.

Eight years later, Peter Singer's *Animal Liberation*, featuring a vicious chapter on the evils of animal research, became the bible of a new animal movement. Suddenly, animal welfare was out, and animal rights was in.

Singer's blaze burst into a firestorm when a young reader of *Animal Liberation* went to work in a laboratory at the Institute for Behavioral Research in Silver Spring, Maryland. There, Edward Taub was conducting NIH-funded research aimed at providing more complete rehabilitation for victims of strokes and spinal cord injuries. Nine monkeys, in which the sensory nerves in the arms had been painlessly severed, were being trained to use their nonfeeling limbs. Alex

Pacheco led police and animal control officers on a mission to rescue them.

The rest of the story is now a tangle of allegations about what took place in the laboratory and what subsequently happened to the "rescued" monkeys. Though trials and investigations have left questions about the photos taken by Pacheco, the image of a monkey writhing in an apparatus that looks like a torture device—along with the message "This Is Vivisection"— became the poster for research cruelty.

Apart from this "scandal" and unresolved mystery as well as Singer's book, a satisfactory explanation for the spectacular success of the animal rights movement probably lies in a combination of several factors:

- *Charismatic leadership.* Ingrid Newkirk, who joined Pacheco to found P*e*TA, is a master of the modern sound bite. She has built P*e*TA into an organization of hundreds of thousands of members with an annual budget of thirty-three to thirty-five million dollars. With her media savvy, she has made the name of P*e*TA into household shorthand for concern for animals.
- *The media.* The contemporary communications industry has made entertainers into role models and the evening news into entertainment. Alicia Silverstone, Kim Basinger, and Alec Baldwin have become authorities more trusted than scientists. TV stations, nervously following the sweeps, now deliver sensational stories of disasters and sentimental stories of animals much more frequently than any hard reporting of the more important events and policies that are shaping our lives.
- *Feminism.* A statistic is telling: women made up 68 percent of the 1990 March for Animals participants (Jamison, 445). Evidently, women see a connection between their exploitation and the alleged suffering of laboratory animals. For animal rights philosopher Mary Midgely, a crossover of feminists to animal rights organizations is not surprising because both movements critique male institutions and attitudes (Sperling, 145–46). The medical and research establishment is still predominately male in its makeup and—so reads the script—cold, compartmentalized, and rational in its methods.
- *Prosperity.* Researchers invited to speak in countries of exploding populations, anemic economies, weak educational systems, poor

nutrition, and scarce health care seldom observe animal activism. It is remarkable, too, that in this country animal rights protests are usually made up of whites, with little representation from Asians, Hispanics, or African Americans. It seems that to some extent prosperity and material comfort release energies that people turn to animal welfare and, sometimes, animal activism.

- *Urbanization.* In colonial America and Europe before the 1900s, everyone lived near animals—horses, cows, rabbits, and wolves. We shared the environment with them and understood their natures, suffering, and needs. Now, 80 percent of the population of the United States lives in cities and suburbs. Most of us grow up with little experience of farm animals, let alone with animals in the wild. Our only experiences with real animals are with pets—in that 1990 March for Animals, 87 percent of the marchers indicated that an intensely emotional experience with a pet was a significant mobilizing force in their lives (Jamison, 445).

- *Entertainment.* What urbanization has taken away—firsthand experience of real animals—Disney has replaced. Children today experience animals not only as pets but also as animated cartoon characters. Mickey Mouse, Bambi, Babe, and Spirit, adorable creatures that reciprocate human expressions of fear and sorrow, curiosity and glee, evoke deep affection for the real creatures they represent.

- *Distrust of science.* Science writer Jon Franklin believes that the animal rights movement is thriving in an atmosphere of hostility to science. Scientists may point to technological developments that have made our lives easier, if not better, but contemporary Cassandras remind us of Chernobyl and warn us about holes in the ozone layer, pesticides in the food chain, the disastrous heating of our global home, and the possibility of a brave new world created by cloning and genetic engineering. Resentment has been growing to what many label empirical, invasive, and soulless research.

- *Medical advances.* Lack of trust in science and technology would not be as powerful a factor as it is, were it not for present-day forgetfulness of the role that animal research has played in our health. Because of the successes of biomedical research we speak of the "miracles" of modern medicine, overlooking the origins of these miracles in decades of gradually acquired information, much of it garnered through animal research. Show a group of junior high school students a picture of iron lungs lined up in rows in the children's wing of a hospital, and only one or two of them, if you are lucky, will know what those contraptions are; most of the rest will not have heard of the polio epidemic that terrified parents and their children in the 1950s. This historical amnesia renders us vulnerable to claims of animal activists that no good comes of animal research.

Charismas and celebrities, media and entertainment, feminism and accelerating urbanization, renewed distrust of science and technology, and, perhaps most important, forgetfulness of the achievements of biomedical research all contribute to the rise and success of the contemporary animal rights movement. These cultural developments provide a context, a "right" moment, a favorable climate for the animal rights movement.

What explains the making of an animal extremist? Some animal extremists claim that their dedication is a logical extension of the passion for justice that marked the 1960s. Or, it could be that animal rights extremism arises from the disillusionment that followed the collapse of earlier civil rights and antiwar movements. Gen-Xers are noted for their cynicism and disdain for mainstream politics. Many young people today have given up on humans, but feel affection and compassion for animals because animals, at least, live in innocence.

As distrust of ideology and institutions has led in the last few years to disgust for politicians, media, bankers, financial analysts, auditors, and clergy, the theme of animal innocence appears more and more. A few years ago we were part of a movie audience that sat silent and mesmerized while watching gangland shootings. Then it gasped collectively and in horror when a frog was apparently garroted. That reaction brought to mind a comment made by an extremist and quoted by *New York Newsday* columnist B. D. Colen: "Unlike you [human being that you are], the cockroach has never done anything deliberately malicious in its life—unlike every human that ever lived. I actually have more moral grounds to murder you, than you have to, say, swat a fly" (Colen).

Idealism, especially the youthful variety, will always find an outlet. Like Mark Rudd, who "liberated" the office of a college president in the 1960s, like Daniel Berrigan, who in the same years poured blood on draft files, like the Unabomber, animal extremists are idealists turned revolutionaries. They are convent school alums and altar boys, Peace Corps veterans and self-taught religious scholars. Their intense idealism has found a constituency—innocent animals—that is above reproach and will never disappoint their dream of a better world.

In some senses, the animal rights movement is, as Yogi Berra is supposed to have said, "*Dejá vu* all over again." A vigorous antivivisection movement nearly brought a halt to nineteenth-century physiological research in England. Fortunately, scientists succeeded in recruiting the powerful medical profession to carry the standard of research, and the British Medical Association persuaded Parliament to pass a bill that regulated rather than ended animal research.

No one could wish for new plagues to bring home to the public the need for animal research and put animal extremism to rest. Yet, with global warming, jet travel, bird flu, and AIDS, as well as threats of bio-terrorists, diseases once unknown or once thought to be conquered are arriving on our doorstep. It may be that exotic and resurgent viruses will swing public opinion in favor of animal research. But, if what happened in England 150 years ago provides any lesson, it is this: medical schools, scientific societies, physician organizations, and research institutions must get out and explain the connection between animal research and human and animal health. We cannot afford to keep animal research a dirty little secret.

PETER SINGER: FATHER OF THE ANIMAL RIGHTS MOVEMENT

Two surprises: first, Peter Singer doesn't have a particular affection for animals (Singer [1], x). Second, this reputed father of the animal rights movement doesn't believe in rights. Instead, he follows Jeremy Bentham (1748–1832), in saying that ethical reflection arises from our empathy with others in their pleasure or pain. When ethics is based on calculations of pleasure and pain, it includes responsibilities not just to rational humans, but also to any creatures that experience pleasure and pain. Singer quotes a Bentham proclamation that has become "The Great Sentence" of the animal rights movement: "The question is not, Can they reason? nor Can they talk? but, Can they suffer?" (Hearne, 60).

Bentham proposed that we align ourselves with a hypothetical observer who is impartial, benevolent, and capable of discerning every consequence of a given action. From such a position we would be able to choose actions that achieve the greatest utility—defined as the maximum pleasure and minimum pain—for the greatest number of individuals. In our calculations, or course, individuals must be weighed equally.

Singer extends Bentham's method to animals. He doesn't claim that humans and animals are equal or demand that we treat them equally. Most members of the chromosomal species *homo sapiens* are persons—they possess rationality and self-consciousness—but most animals are not. Conversely, some chromosomal humans, such as the mentally disadvantaged and senile, are not persons, while some animals such as chimpanzees clearly are (Singer [3]). Persons or not, all suffer. Consequently, even though we need not treat each sentient creature equally we must consider the potential pleasures and pains of each equally as we ponder how to treat them. If we give special consideration to certain individuals solely on the basis of their membership in the human species we act as "speciesists." Singer concludes: "If the experimenter is not prepared to use an orphaned human infant, then his readiness to use nonhumans is simple discrimination, since adult apes, cats, mice, and other mammals are more aware of what is happening to them, more self-directing and, so far as we can tell, at least as sensitive to pain, as any human infant" (Singer [2], 81–82).

If the outcomes of pleasure and pain determine what is right, we may ask how we are to judge experiments, even those that end in death, on anesthetized subjects. Here Singer counsels us to consider not just pleasures and pains, but also the interests and harms of those we affect. We best determine interests and harms by taking into account what would be individuals' preferences. It is safe to say that no sentient subject would choose to be experimented on or killed, no matter how painless the procedures. Singer allows "because human pleasures are fuller and human futures richer, the harm and the wrong involved in overriding preferences is usually greater with humans than with animals." Nevertheless, the rule-of-thumb test remains in place: If the pleasures and interests of some human infants are no greater than those of many animals, then "we must, if we intend to experiment on and kill animals, be prepared to do the same to those babies" (Singer [2], 21). It is not hard to see that Singer's utilitarian approach provides a perfect launching pad for scathing attacks on most every use of animals. Chapters of *Animal Liberation* on the cruelty of eating meat, raising farm animals, clothing oneself in furs and leather, and entertaining oneself at zoos and circuses set the agenda for animal liberation. Most famous, however, is chapter 2, which catalogues the evils of biomedical research.

If chapter 2 of *Animal Liberation* is still today the bible for those who want to end biomedical research, then a long rebuttal by Sharon Russell and Charles Nicoll is an important and balancing commentary (Russell and Nicoll, 109–39). Examining Singer's text verse-by-verse, case-by-case, these authors find that he has presented a caricature of research. They contend, moreover, that instead of rigorous utilitarian calculations Singer gives us nothing but blanket assertions equating animal research with animal cruelty and writing off "much of it [as] of minimal or zero value" (Singer [2], 36). Russell and Nicoll note that Singer "makes virtually no attempt to consider objectively the benefits that have been realized from animal-based medical research, and he greatly exaggerates the costs." They add, "To him, animal research is 'all pain and no gain'" (Russell and Nicoll, 109).

Singer's bias may disappoint, but it should not surprise. Long before Russell and Nicoll, critics of utilitarian ethics pointed out that it is usually impossible for us to quantify, measure, and compare various pleasures and pains and interests that might or might not be served by alternative courses of action. Utilitarianism turns out to be an especially poor guide in the enterprise of discovery that is basic biomedical research. Scientists in basic research seek to reveal the unknown. They have no completed picture to guide their work. They make connections, often serendipitously, between seemingly unrelated pieces of information, connections that open up new dimensions of incompleteness and new directions for inquiry. Scientists are explorers, not clairvoyants.

Singer himself proves how this criticism hits the mark. Ten years after declaring that the routine use of hundreds of thousands of laboratory animals in research "without the remotest prospect of significant benefits for human beings or any other animals" is ethically unacceptable, he heralded research in which experimentally damaged nervous systems of rats were repaired with stem cells derived from embryos (Singer [5]). Singer touted these experiments because they could lead to the practice of growing tissues for the repair or replacement of damaged organs, thus eliminating the need of temporary animal transplants for patients on human organ waiting lists. He ignored the fact, however, that these experiments depended on decades of basic research, much of it conducted with little glimmer of its role in stem cell therapy and all of it involving the routine use of thousands of laboratory rats. None of it would have been approved, if Singer's moral calculus had been used prospectively.

Similarly but more recently, Singer gave his *nihil obstat* to primate research on Parkinson's disease. To Oxford scientist Tipu Aziz, who asked him to weigh improvements in health already enjoyed by forty thousand human patients against the harms—the nature of the harms was unspecified—to one hundred monkey subjects, Singer said, "Well, I think if you put a case like that, clearly I would have to agree that that was a justifiable experiment" (Walsh). Again, Singer's utilitarian calculation ignored the basic research that preceded and made possible Dr. Aziz's contribution. Moreover, his approval came with all the advantages of hindsight; it couldn't, as moral judgments must, guide Dr. Aziz when he was setting out on research that had no certain outcome. One doesn't have to be a scientist to be a critic of Singer. In fact, his arguments provoke several lines of criticism (Berkowitz, 34; Carruthers, 9), even from another animal rights philosopher (Regan [2]).

We have mentioned that Singer would allow using animals for health research as long as scientists are also ready to use marginal human infants. This stipulation understandably causes revulsion. Forthright and with steely resolve, Singer strives to overcome that such revulsion. He reportedly argues that parents should have the right to end the lives not just of fetuses, but also of severely disabled infants, a class that includes hemophiliac and Down's syndrome babies (Berkowitz). He really could live in a world in which parents make decisions about who lives and who dies and in which scientists use defective infants in laboratory experiments.

Most people, however, find something special in human beings, whether impaired or not. James Lindemann Nelson notes that "The birth of a "marginal" human, or the reduction of a normal human to a marginal state, is a tragedy; the birth of, say, a healthy collie pup, whose potentials are roughly on a par with the human's, is not" (Nelson, 192). The grief and the pity we experience in the presence of marginal humans reveal that we view them quite differently than animals, who lack the same potentials but whom we happily accept as normal.

Let's assume that scientists were ready to join Singer in using marginal human infants in place of animals. A difficulty would remain, and surely Singer is not so naïve as to fail recognizing it. The occasional defective child disposed for medical research would hardly satisfy the need for the thousands of laboratory animals that are carefully designed, produced, and used by biomedical researchers to model physiological processes, including disease. Perhaps the key word for Singer is "ready": scientists should be "ready" to use defective children when such are appropriate and available to the research at hand. It is hard to see, however, how such readiness, most often a mental state never resulting in the experimental use of a human subject, would contribute much to the liberation of animals from their alleged suffering in research laboratories. In the end, Singer's stipulation would be effective in only one way—as a condition that could never be met and which would therefore bring a lasting halt to animal research.

Who said that philosophy doesn't count in the real world of our daily lives?

DRAMATIS PERSONAE: ORGANIZATIONS AND PERSONS

A quick Google search will reveal that there are thousands of animal organizations worldwide. They range the political spectrum, from traditional welfare societies to newcomer extremist groups. They include reasonable groups—ones that work only to spay and neuter feral (wild) animals to prevent them from overpopulating and endangering other species or risking starvation—and gatherings of the most wild-eyed, people—those who promise that if you wear leather, eat meat, or support medical research or zoos, they will do everything possible, legal and illegal, to stop you.

The point here is twofold. First, there is something for everyone, a group and an agenda to match your particular interest. But, and this is the second point, if your way of participating is to contribute money, you may discover that you are supporting more than just the organization of your choice with its very reasonable agenda. Funds can move between groups.

PeTA

We have already met the largest (PeTA) and the most aggressive of the organizations (ALF/ELF and SHAC), but since military tacticians strongly advise that you respect your enemy and understand his strengths, these organizations invite a little more investigation. In 1980, Ingrid Newkirk and Alex Pacheco founded PeTA, an organization that today boasts well over seven hundred thousand members. P*e*TA is dedicated to establishing and protecting animal rights. It has an annual budget of thirty-three to thirty-five million dollars, but don't expect much of that money to be used to feed and house strays or unwanted animals or to sterilize wild animals to prevent further breeding. It is well documented that at least some of the money it collects for helping animals is used, if not in mass mailings that solicit even more money, to support persons and groups with quite different agendas (Better Business Bureau). One analysis of P*e*TA's required IRS filings has been performed by the Better Business Bureau. It outlines the use of its income and notes certain omissions of what are called best practices in philanthropy (Better Business Bureau).

Lewiston Morning Tribune writer Michael Costello asks us to "Follow P*e*TA money to domestic terrorism." He lists three questionable recipients of P*e*TA largesse:

- $45,000 to convicted ALF member Rodney Coronado's legal defense
- $2,000 to national ALF spokesperson David Wilson
- $1,500 to the Earth Liberation Front

Costello notes:

> The FBI calls ELF "the largest and most active U.S.-based terrorist group." That group is responsible for many tens of millions of dollars in damage.
> So far, the ELF hasn't killed anyone, but they don't shrink from the possibility. "While innocent life will never be harmed in any action we undertake, where it is necessary we will no longer hesitate to pick up the gun to implement justice," declared an ELF spokesman after one attack. (Costello)

ALF/ ELF and SHAC

ALF/ELF and SHAC are organized in a truly remarkable way. The groups refer to themselves as cells and operate with virtual autonomy. A captured soldier provides only name, rank, and serial number. If a captured soldier discloses all he knows—other plans, identities and locations—he gives the enemy an advantage. This won't happen to animal extremist groups. The totally independent operating cells are fully ignorant of other cells' plans, membership, location or intentions. If caught, they can tell nothing, because they know nothing (CBS [3]).

To terrorize effectively, these cells have to make the threat known to the public. Someone must tell the story. For this, as we have seen with Craig Rosebraugh, extremists have invented the independent "press office." Whenever a "direct action" occurs, the action is announced by the press office. Because the press office doesn't directly participate in the action it may, legally, even applaud the effort. If asked, the press office simply notes that it received an anonymous fax or encrypted email that cannot be traced. The email system is manipulated via anonymous servers that mask the source of the message, and Pretty Good Protection (PGP) keys provide message encryption from all but the intended recipient.

Independent Media, or "Indymedia," as it is known, further supports the press offices. Type "Indymedia" into search engines, and you will get over thirty million hits. Indymedia defines itself as "a collective of independent media organizations and hundreds of journalists offering grassroots, non-corporate coverage . . . a democratic media outlet for the creation of radical, accurate, and passionate tellings of truth (Independent Media [1]).

Listservs (self-subscribed email lists that regularly deliver news information directly to the recipients' email boxes) augment the dissemination of animal extremist doctrines and reports of terrorizing direct actions.

These outlets serve as news pollinators. Operating in many languages and carrying information about respectable political and economic justice causes, they are read by audiences much larger than the counter-culture community. Conventional media representatives mine their articles for story leads. The power of these outlets to disseminate news and call activists to arms can't be overestimated.

Animal extremists are deceptively well organized and, in spite of their cell operation with its advantageous deniability, they are well informed and well integrated. So well organized is the ALF that it published a report in 2001 of the actions in which it had participated. It contained a detailed inventory of the "animals liberated" up to and including "one snail." Copyrighted and running forty-seven pages, the document resembled, both in detail and in pride of presentation, the "Report to Shareholders" of a major corporation (North American Animal Liberation Front).

So remarkable is the operation of "press offices" that the FBI twice raided the home and operations center of the one in the United States, but failed to recover sufficient information to immediately pursue arrests. The Royal Canadian Mounted Police raided a parallel operation in Canada with the same result (Donohue).

The animal movement's integration is manifested when a partisan is arrested. Immediately a statement is placed on Web sites, Listservs, and other outlets, protesting innocence and remarking that his or her arrest is further evidence of illegal and oppressive government action. The announcement appeals for phone calls, faxes, and emails to the jurisdiction in which the person is being held. And this works. Hundreds of members of shadowy terrorists groups as well as legitimate animal welfare organizations swing into action.

Americans love to sign petitions. People will put their names to virtually anything that doesn't cost them money, even if they do not know the specifics of the cause. One Web site, catering to animal rightists and other causes, is neatly indexed by topic/cause and creates an online medium for collecting signatures. It gives the appearance of having a large following. Although extremists do not operate this particular site, they are able to use it as a convenient tool.

Like several animal rights organizations, SHAC raises money from well-meaning people who wind up unwittingly funding violence. Jo-Ann Goodwin, writing in the *Daily Mail* of London reports that SHAC runs innocent-looking High Street stalls throughout the country, raising funds from passersby who have no conception that the group will stop at nothing to secure its aims (Goodwin).

PCRM

Other smaller, less aggressive organizations are also of interest. Often, their names are chosen to confuse and obscure purpose. Notice, too, that groups frequently select self-aggrandizing names that include words like "Coalition," "Modernization," "Physicians," "Students," "Institute," or aspects of social helpfulness such as "change," "fairness," or "mercy." In one case, the appeal is to our age's sense of doom and urgency about the environment: Hollywood soap actor Chris DeRose's Last Chance for Animals.

The Physician's Committee for Responsible Medicine, led by Neal Barnard, MD, sounds like a *bona fide* independent and professional medical group. It turns out that less than 10 percent of PCRM membership consists of physicians and that it receives funding from The Foundation to Support Animal Protection, an organization that evidently funds various charitable, educational, and scientific groups including P*e*TA and PCRM (Carmichael).

"Responsible medicine" is code for an agenda promoting diets and medical practices not dependent on animals. In recent years, PCRM seems to have taken up cudgels from the Medical Research Modernization Committee whose chairman, Stephen Kaufman, MD, frequently teams up with Barnard in authoring articles that oppose animal research.

Not long after PCRM was performing its public service of informing the public that milk is dangerous and should not be recommended in the government's nutrition guidelines, the senior vice president of the American Medical Association noted, "The AMA continues to marvel at how effectively a fringe organization of questionable repute continues to hoodwink the media with a series of questionable research that fails to enhance public health. . . . The Physicians Committee for Responsible Medicine is an animal 'rights' organization, and, despite its title, represents less than 0.5 percent of the total U.S. physician population" (Center for Consumer Freedom).

As with the organization, so with Barnard, its leader—what you see isn't exactly what you get. According to the bio he has written for WEBMD, he is a nutrition researcher and adjunct associate professor of medicine at George Washington University School of Medicine in Washington, DC. He is the author of seven books on diet and health, and his research has been published in the *American Journal of Cardiology*, *Obstetrics & Gynecology*, and *Preventive Medicine*. He is also editor-in-chief of *Good Medicine* and the author of hundreds of articles in magazines such as *Scientific American* and newspapers such as the *New York Times*. Barnard is a regular guest on network news and talk shows and an active public speaker.

This bio withholds some critical facts. Barnard trained as a psychiatrist, not a neuroscientist or a nutritionist. He is closely connected to P*e*TA in more than funding: he has served as its "Science Advisor" (ActivistCash [4]). Of his "hundreds" of articles, most of the twenty-eight medical journal articles listed on the National Library of Medicine's resource PUBMED, as of August 29, 2004, like his newspaper pieces and editorials, communicated his dietary suggestions and beliefs about the deceptions of animal research—not any scientific research (PUBMED).

Moviegoers in the fall of 2004 saw Barnard star as a "science expert" in *Supersize Me*. As audiences washed away popcorn with thirty-ounce soft drinks, he explained to them how the brain's reward circuits addict them to fast foods and junk foods. It is likely that the audiences didn't realize that what scientists know about those circuits has been learned through the research that Barnard, when wearing his animal rights hat, so vigorously opposes.

Recently, Jerry Vlasak, MD, has garnered a good deal of publicity for PCRM, all of it concerning its real agenda of animal rights. In the fall of 2004, this PCRM member was barred from entering the United Kingdom because he had been quoted as saying that millions of animal lives could be saved if a handful of researchers were killed (BBC [2]). Vlasak denied making the comment, but did assert, under media questioning, that violence against scientists is "morally acceptable." Of course, he clarified that he did not personally advocate violence against scientists involved in animal experiments, but only believe that it "may be useful" in the battle for animal liberation (BBC [3]).

Another name that was probably chosen to confuse is the Humane Society of the United States (HSUS). It is important to distinguish HSUS and local humane societies that run animal shelters. HSUS, unlike local humane societies, doesn't run a single animal shelter—a fact that would surprise many of its donors. Instead it spends tens of millions of dollars opposing modern livestock and poultry farming, circuses, and dog breeding. Many humane society leaders look wistfully at donations that HSUS is getting from well-meaning people who intend them for animal welfare, not animal activism.

Names that mean pretty much what they say include the American Anti-Vivisection Society, which leads the campaign against dissection in schools; the National Anti-Vivisection Society, one of the oldest animal organizations in the United States; and the New England Anti-Vivisection Society (NEAVS). During the 1980s, P*e*TA succeeded in getting Neal Barnard and some of its own members on the NEAVS board, and subsequently monies began flowing in the direction of PCRM (ActivistCash [4]).

IDA, ALDF, and the Animal Protection Institute

Other large and influential national organizations include In Defense of Animals, which employs both Matt Rossell and Rick Bogle and leads the continuing attack on the Oregon National Primate Research Center; the Animal Legal Defense Fund (ALDF), which called for the USDA inspection that— alas for it—exonerated the ONPRC; and the Animal Protection Institute of America, which organized a national letter-writing campaign that brought the center mail from hundreds of "outraged" but misinformed citizens.

Local Organizations

On the local scene, organizations multiply. In Oregon we have seen, in addition to local chapters of IDA and ALDF, the Coalition Against Animal Testing (led by Craig Rosebraugh's companion, Elaine Close), Coalition Against Primate Experimentation and Research (CAPER), People for Animal Rights, Rodent Alliance for Tolerance (now called Rat Allies and run by Roger Troen, who was convicted of "liberating" three hundred rats, cats, and rabbits from a University of Oregon lab in 1986) and Students for the Ethical Treatment of Animals.

Locally grown groups sometimes graduate to national presence. A case in point is Rick Bogle's Primate Freedom Project, which stages demonstrations at primate centers around the country. It has taken over responsibility for the monkey tag fundraiser (see chapter 4) invented by Bogle's earlier organization, the Coalition to End Primate Experimentation. Other groups, such as the Laboratory Primate Advocacy Group, rise to one occasion—it tried to organize animal technicians to protest our institution in 2000—and then seem to disappear.

The key to understanding the groups is the fact that many are intertwined, based on personal relationships—Nedim Buyukmihci, DVM, co-founder of Veterinarians for Animal Rights, and Kim Sturla, director of companion animal issues and education for Fund for the Animals, were, until recently, husband and wife, for example—cross-advertising, overlapping membership, and Web sites that frequently operate through the same servers.

The SHAC-USA president is, at the time we are writing this, Pamela Ferdin, RN. Her husband is PCRM spokesman Jerry Vlasak. Ferdin's business cards affiliate her with PCRM, but use the business address of the Animal Defense League of Los Angeles, an aggressive protest group run by Ferdin, Vlasak, and PeTA's in-school lecturer Gary Yourofsky, the guy who started my problems in Florida. Sometimes you feel like you are playing, "Three Points of Separation!"

One group makes an allegation; others quote it as truth. Then an activist surfing the Web and reading about the allegation from all the many sites—could so many people be wrong?—accepts it as true and sends it out to all on his Listserv. Later, when evidence from independent investigations demonstrates the untruth of the allegation, he fails to notice, or chooses to ignore the uncomfortable news.

In the United States we promote the idea that each voice must be heard and weighed equally. The animal rightist world has learned that, with each new free Yahoo! or Hotmail account, a new voice is developed. A whole Web site only costs thirty dollars; each one is the appearance of a new group, a suggestion of a groundswell of activity; in reality, they are just colored images on a screen.

Proresearch Groups

How about proresearch groups? The truth is that there are not many. Sometimes grateful patients band together and send scientists supportive letters, and there are a few groups that lobby for federal support and more research. Seriously ill patients seldom have the strength to lobby for life-saving medical research. Christopher Reeve and his foundation has been a notable exception in this regard.

The Foundation for Biomedical Research (FBR) engages in educational outreach, and its sister organization, the National Association for Biomedical Research (NABR), conducts lobbying efforts. Industry groups include an effective media and lobbying resource, Americans for Medical Progress (AMP), an Alexandria, Virginia, group supported by pharmaceutical companies. The National Animal Interest Alliance, which supports business, agricultural, scientific, and recreational interests, has been formed to protect and promote humane practices and relationships between people and animals. A more recent player is the Center for Consumer Freedom, funded by restaurateurs who recognize that their industry is just one of several under attack from animal rightists. The Fur Commission USA looks after the interests of mink farmers whose animals were routinely stolen and abandoned in the wild by extremists, many now in jail.

Budgets of aboveground animal rights organizations in 2002–2003 totaled $167 million; budgets of FBR and NABR came to slightly more than $2 million. Animal extremist groups, which a casual observer might think are ragtag operations, draw strength from their lack of structure and shadowy leadership; proresearch organizations are hampered as they play by the rules and in the open daylight of regulatory disclosure. The playing field is hardly level.

CHAPTER 4

ANIMAL RIGHTS STRATEGIES

Let's say, just for the purpose of this chapter, that you hate us for what we do. Let's also say that our neighbor loves us, because of the good work that we do in advancing the well-being of humankind's health and even on behalf of the animals that benefit from animal research. Now, what can you do to get us to stop what we do and to change that neighbor's point of view? First, allege, without evidence or first-hand knowledge, that

- animal researchers produce nothing of value because animals are too different from humans to produce useful models of humans;
- animal researchers torture animals because: (a) they derive pleasure from it, (b) they make lots of money at it, and (c) they have no love of animals and are intrinsically unkind and cruel—sort of like Nazis.

When you have everyone's attention—and, possibly, their sympathy, too—start planning the worst things that you can do or persuade someone to do in your stead that are either (a) legal or (b) illegal but not likely to get you caught and that you can blame on unnamed extremists.

Exercise your right of free speech. Try to convince others that you are have the right point of view about us and that we need to be put out of business. Get on the radio, give public talks, try to get people to debate you, publish letters to the editor, put handbills on cars. So far, no legal problems. This falls under the category that animal rightists call "asking nicely."

The problem, as P*e*TA's Newkirk has reportedly pointed out, is that your efforts so far are not really effective. "Our non-violent tactics are not as effective. We ask nicely for years and get nothing. Someone makes a threat, and it works" (Berman). She is correct: statistics say that most people will ignore you since they *do* support animal research, especially if they know about the regulations that are in place to safeguard the well-being of the animals.

So you have to up the ante. Still mindful of the law, you come to my neighborhood and pass fliers out to my neighbors. You spice them up a bit with some grainy pictures that you get off the Internet, never really suggesting, of course, that those horrific images actually came from my lab. In fact, you don't know where they came from. You add my picture (obtained from the university's Web site), include my home address (from the public phone directory), and phone number (same source), and the information about where my laboratory is located (also *gratis* of the Web site), hoping that my neighbors will be outraged and drum me out of the neighborhood, stop talking to me—or do something even worse. Maybe you can recruit other activists to call me at work and upset me.

You say in the flier that I am a cruel vivisector. So far: "no go." It just doesn't work; there is no instantaneous public outcry. So you and ten of your friends show up at my house, about 8:30 PM after the kids are asleep, and start beating on trashcan lids and chanting something like, "*Hey, hey, ho, ho . . . animal research has got to go.*" You repeat this enough to wake the kids and get the dog barking. You leave, convinced that this is all legal—and in some jurisdictions it is—depending on the volume and timing of the noise. Now the neighbors are walking over to my house and asking me what is going on. You are starting to see some success.

You return in a week and repeat the process. No barking dogs this time because we are on vacation. "Damn, wasted evening and the police got called by disturbed neighbors." The police tell you that you can protest, but you have to be quiet and you have to come and leave before 10:00 PM. Doesn't that mess things up—how can you get attention without making noise—especially if I am not in the house to harass?

A week goes by. You come back and decide to come to my door. You beat on it—after all, you are indignant. The dog barks. I look out the window and see ten people standing there in odd costumes and in silence holding candles and posters. Since it is not Halloween, I decide not to open the door. So far, what you've done is legal in my state. People can exercise free speech and even walk up my sidewalk and knock on the door—unless I put up "No Trespassing" and "No Soliciting" signs. (The signs have to be a certain size and spaced every twenty feet. Wouldn't that look nice in front of the house and give me the appearance of being a normal person?) What about my right to the quiet and peaceful enjoyment of my home? A policeman tells me that has to be weighed against your right to expression.

Instead of posting signs, I hand you a document drawn up by my attorney (yes, I had to pay for this) that says you are not welcome. Now you can't come up to my door, but the silent vigils in front of the house continue weekly.

You decide to make similar visits to a couple of my colleagues, whom you also declare "vivisectors." You can get into this business; these visits make nice social events.

In order to publicize your "home visits," you post a "story" on the local counterculture Web site. The story need not be true, and of course it isn't subject to any editorial review. A real story, lifted from a real Web site, serves as a model (Independent Media Center).

It reports a visit to a researcher's home by activists dressed as monkeys in jail suits and scientists in lab coats. It describes the arrival of police and asserts that "Both the cops and the protesters think the strong stench of booze on the researcher's breathe [sic] had something to do with her inability to identify the one who rang the doorbell." Adding threat to slur, it concludes,

This is just the beginning Sandy. We are going to change the ways of secrecy in animal research. We are going to show the public what there [sic] tax dollars are going to and remind them what there [sic] not going to. . . . We will be back Sandy. We will go to other houses to [sic]. We wont [sic] quit. Your gonna [sic] have to stop killing monkeys if you want this to end. We are not gonna [sic] be satisfied with unmet promises of coffee and Internet dialogue. See you next time.

You will have set up the Web site to allow discussion by readers. It's a bit clumsy, but it's really worth the trouble. You really want this kind of stuff:

Good for you guys. . . . You dudes really are my heroes. Signed, A Fan

Thanks for standing up for the animals and continuing to bring attention to this issue. This is what is working all over the globe—not letting the vivisectors and financial supporters of animal torture clock out at the end of the day and enjoy their blood money without community pressure. You stand up for the innocent at risk to yourselves, and nothing is more noble than that. Signed, You Protesters are Amazing. (Independent Media Center)

By the time it is "over" you may get the nearly 160 comments to this story. Hey, you're doing great! In reading the posts, though, I was wondering why none of the 160 posts signed a real name. And why there were no phone numbers or street or even emails addresses. And why, when I try to post a reply from a university IP address, the system locks me out.

But you are clearly on a roll, and two or three people you didn't know, sixteen-year-olds, are showing up at your silent demonstrations. One brings her puppy—what a great touch!

You like that this is really annoying to me and my colleagues, and that the police tell me not to leave the house and to pull down the shades. Yup, you and your friends have me trapped in my own house.

You post another time on the counterculture Web site, but add my personal details, including a credit card number you found while going through my trash and a picture of one of the kids, taken by you, while she was walking to school—and my office address phone number, fax number, and email address. You use the credit card to make some generous donations, online, of course, to animal rights organizations. Ha! The punishment fits the crime!

You know I am getting hate mail and threatening calls because you are sending emails from an endless number of free Hotmail and Yahoo! accounts; the calls are costing you money, however, since they are being made from pay phones. Two of your email messages mention the Web site, so you know I learn of it.

Because of your belief that I am such a terrible person, you convince one of the impressionable sixteen-year-olds to dump a little red paint, or "activist-blood," on my car parked in the carport. You leave another note on the car with a flyer and post my comings and goings on the Web site, as if you are following me.

You think about mailing me a razor blade, but decide that is too risky . . . for you. So, instead you order me a few pizzas from different delivery companies.

Costs to Date:
Paint: free from the kid's garage
Cost for phone calls: $4
Cost for copying fliers: $12
Results: significant damage and you have established yourself in the community as a serious activist. Priceless!

For $16 you have caused my family and me great pain. You could go for the deluxe $20 package and buy some gasoline and leave it on my porch, but that seems too extravagant, and you forgot to download the instructions from the ALF site before the police made them take it down. Besides, that *is* illegal.

THE CHILDREN'S CRUSADE:
ANIMAL RIGHTS IN OUR SCHOOLS

About eight hundred years ago, thousands of European children set out under the banner of religion to convert people considered to be infidels. Their crusade ended in tragedy when unscrupulous merchants sold them into slavery.

During the past twenty years, thousands of American children have set out under the flag of P*e*TA to make all of us believers in the doctrine of animal rights. P*e*TA's crusade first takes captive the spontaneous, healthy empathy that little children have with pets and other animals and then the natural, rebellious idealism of kids in their teen years. The crusade is an ominous sign of what could be a future made tragic by the loss of biomedical research.

P*e*TA's leader, Ingrid Newkirk, has said with pride, "We're press sluts" (Specter). She has promoted veganism by comparing the eating of meat to participating in the Holocaust. She has defended P*e*TA grants to extremists convicted of crimes. There is reason for concern about P*e*TA's presence in our schools. Here's a report card for P*e*TA educational efforts:

Behavior 101

Kids arriving at an elementary school find a man costumed as a giant vegetable and identified as Chris P. Carrot, dancing on the sidewalk (Matthews).

They line up for his freebies—barf bags that they are urged to leave on the lunchroom tables for any classmates who eat their animal friends, and animal cartoons featuring cows and an invitation to write a poem on the topic, "How would you feel if a cow ate you?" (P*e*TA).

Chris P. Carrot, who, according to P*e*TA's claim, ran as its 2004 candidate for U.S. President, and barf bags play nicely with children, who love animation and are fascinated by yucky things (P*e*TA Blog). The whole act invites the kids to join P*e*TA in a frequent middle school game—making fun of others. It also softens them up for the bottom line, which will be delivered when they are older: it is wrong to use animals in biomedical research. Vegetarianism might not have a cost, but abstaining from medical treatments and knowledge does. In effect, P*e*TA is enlisting kids in a crusade that is dangerous to their health and ours.

Introduction to Communication

A P*e*TA member sends her child off to middle school with a "gift" for the teacher, a handful of copies of the latest issue of *Grrr! Kids Bite Back* magazine with all its suggestions of lesson plans, art projects, and fun activities that inculcate compassion for animals. Included, of course, is the Web address for a slick online version of the publication.

P*e*TA and other animal rights organizations have caught on that harried teachers, often having large classes and meager resources, welcome ideas for activities and reports and debates that will engage their students.

One idea, of course, is letter writing. At our center, we recently received letters from sixth-grade students whose teacher had taken them on a tour of a primate facility in another state. While on the tour, the teacher had discovered the monkey-tag project of the Committee to End Primate Experimentation. Mimicking the POW "dog tags" that were sold to bring attention to the plight of American POWs in Vietnam, monkey tags bear the ID number of a monkey in one of the nation's primate research centers. Those who buy the tags are encouraged to write for information about the welfare of "their" monkey.

What could be a better project than having all the kids write us? The project integrated zoology, ethics, civics, and English composition. So it was that we got a sheaf of letters about monkey #14396, most of them begging us to release the monkey and stop our "torture" of monkeys. We felt they deserved a reply:

Dear Students:

First, we would like to report that monkey #14396 at the Oregon National Primate Research Center is doing very well. In fact, she is 24 years old!

We put an exclamation point after that last sentence because rhesus monkeys in their habitats in India and Nepal rarely live past 20. Here, where the monkeys receive nutritious daily meals, have an annual physical exam, and get their teeth cleaned regularly, many monkeys live into their 30s. If you would like to see what type of houses monkeys here live in and how they are cared for by specially trained veterinarians and veterinary assistants, look at our Web site (http://onprc.ohsu .edu) on the pages devoted to "Caring for our animals."

You may want to know what we are learning from monkey #14396 and other elders like her. Each day she takes part in memory and learning games. It turns out that older monkeys, just like older humans, learn things and remember things more slowly than youngsters. You've heard of that in the case of humans—we oldsters have trouble working CD players and we're not very good at computer games or even at remembering names. Scientists hope that someday they may learn things about what goes on in the brain as monkeys and humans grow older.

The day that we received your letters one of us heard that a polio epidemic had broken out in the African countries of Nigeria and Burkina-Faso. When we were your age, polio struck fear in every family in this country. In 1956, scientists, who had worked over 50 years with monkeys to learn how the poliovirus infects people, found out how to protect people with a vaccine. Today, in this country, thanks to research with monkeys, you and I don't have to worry about polio. We think that you hope, as we hope, that doctors can get that vaccine to the children in Africa very quickly.

There are many things that scientists learn about health and disease—not just human health and disease, but animal health and disease as well—through animal research. You may want to study illnesses that we are researching at this center such as multiple sclerosis, diabetes, and AIDS. Scientists are dedicated to this work out of their love and concern for people and for animals, and they are happy, as you will be happy to learn, that the monkeys involved in this research are treated very compassionately and very well.

Thank you for your letters and please let us know if you have any more questions.

Advanced Critical Thought

A boy in a high school current affairs class suggests discussion of a billboard he has just seen down the street. The billboard, which spoofs the national "Got milk?" campaign (funded by U.S. milk processors and dairy farmers, the Milk Processor Education Program [MilkPEP], and Dairy Management Inc.) implies that milk is bad for young people and that they should drink beer instead.

Children rarely know enough about the science of nutrition to escape enslavement to misinformation in the anti-milk campaign. Robert P. Heaney, MD, FACP, FACN, Creighton University Professor of Medicine, noted in congressional testimony on the (surprisingly) controversial issue of milk in school lunches:

> I think it is useful to recognize the origin of the anti-milk campaign—and it is literally a campaign. If one checks carefully, one finds that behind most of the stories is an organization called The People for the Ethical Treatment of Animals and its sister organization, the Physicians Committee for Responsible Medicine. These are animal rights organizations that oppose the use of any animal product—leather, fur, meat, or milk. [When the federal government was reviewing its] Dietary Guidelines for Americans, PCRM shamelessly played the race card, alleging that African Americans could not digest milk because of lactose intolerance. The facts are that people of all races are able to consume, digest, and benefit from milk without difficulty. (Heaney)

Life Sciences

In a high school biology lab, a young girl announces to her teacher that she will not be participating in the frog dissection. She saw *Clueless* actress Alicia Silverstone in a TV ad explain, "biology is about life, not death." And she saw an ad in the *Spokane Spokesman Review* newspaper described by journalist Michael Costello:

> [It] attempts to make the case that high school animal dissection labs give us serial killers. [It] recalls that most schools have 'zero tolerance' policies on weapons. It shows a gun and a knife as examples of forbidden weapons. And, it shows a scalpel. . . . According to P*e*TA, using a scalpel to probe the anatomy of a formaldehyde-marinated amphibian is the equivalent of turning a gun on a cafeteria full of school kids. And the advertisement concludes with a reminder that the late serial killer and cannibal, Jeffrey Dahmer, cited his high school biology classes as his inspiration. (Costello)

Whatever one may think about high school dissection labs—some biomedical researchers believe that they are not valuable learning experiences for most high school students—three facts remain: (1) the practice is not cruel; (2) Jeffrey Dahmer notwithstanding, there is no proven connection between dissection and serial murder; and (3) the so-called "alternative" to dissection, computer simulation, is more like Disney World than science. No simulation of a frog dissection can reveal the contents of a real frog's stomach, the record of its breakfast, the one bit of evidence that all animals both eat and are eaten.

Contemporary Communications

The way we communicate and interact is changing at a remarkable pace—email and the Internet have turned faxing into a nearly vanished technology. Web sites like MySpace, Friendster, and Facebook create new venues for social networking—venues quickly occupied by animal rights groups for their advantage. United Press International (UPI) was among the first to identify the new turf. In a story in August 2006, it quoted Jacquie Calnan of Americans for Medical Progress, who noted that MySpace is clearly a great recruiting tool for the demographic of teenagers and young adults. Calnan also noted that animal rights groups have a strong presence on YouTube.com, where they post videos of animal experiments and of activists vandalizing labs. She expressed worry that young people may be particularly susceptible to some of the messages coming from the extremists. "There are folks who really aren't fully mature yet who are seeing this," she says, "and want to make a name among themselves and haven't been exposed to the other side of the issue" (Mitchell [1]).

Getting the pro-animal-research message to young people may require groups such as hers to establish a presence on MySpace and similar sites. But the animal research enterprise may be facing an uphill battle as it competes with already very popular sites carrying pictures and videos, lifted from the context and explanation that would make them perfectly acceptable, of laboratory dogs or monkeys in cages; vandals breaking into labs and releasing animals; or activists carrying out protests.

Will this Web approach successfully recruit and inspire a fourteen-year-old to commit a violent act against a humane animal researcher, spray paint on a car, or make a threatening phone call? It's too early to tell.

The report card: P*e*TA's brain trust and the entire animal rights community gets an "A" for ingenious strategies of bypassing parental supervision and getting through the doors and into the schools, but an "F" for contributions to the education and the well-being of our young people. The trouble, according to M. Sue Benford, executive director of the Ohio Scientific Education & Research Association, is that "Information gets skewed in the spin of those types of [humane] curriculums, and all of a sudden, kids become zealots for a cause that they really don't completely understand—they have never been given the whole picture" (Morano).

National polls reveal that adherence to animal rights beliefs falls off sharply around the age of thirty (Kiefer). It seems that with a little experience in life, especially the experience of having one's own children and aging, comes a tempered wisdom. Still, captivating children in a contradictory and confused ideology is wrong.

It is a wrong that bothers Dennis Edmunds, father of a student at Eisenhower High School in Macomb Township, Michigan. He went on Detroit's WXYZ-TV news to say, "School is not a place to be pushing your political agenda" (WXYZ-TV). He was reacting to learning that his son and six hundred other students had heard Gary Yourofsky, whose views on condoning violence in the name of animal rights we've already encountered, speak at their school. Now a self-described P*e*TA lecturer—P*e*TA pays for his transportation and educational materials—Yourofsky told the students, "When you cause misery to animals and take part in their murder, you are causing misery to God and murdering his soul" (WXYZ-TV).

It sounds very much like a religious crusade. Others make the same connection for school children between animal rights and religion, none more explicitly than lawyer Gary Francione. His *Vivisection and Dissection in the Classroom: A Guide to Conscientious Objection* instructs young people that their animal rights cause is the equivalent of religious belief. He advises young people that conscientious objection to classroom dissection is a constitutionally protected exercise of religious belief. To be protected, their belief need not be in the "Supreme Being" of traditional faiths, but might be more like Yourofsky's "God," the spirit present in every animal. If a belief is a matter of "ultimate concern" and occupies in the lives of its adherents "a place parallel to that filled by . . . God" in traditionally religious persons, then it passes the test for religious belief. "Most animal advocates," he observes, "possess a deeply spiritual commitment to justice for the oppressed and a general revulsion toward violence against sentient beings" (Francione and Charlton, 20). Theirs is a religion by another name.

This children's crusade, even if doesn't retain its recruits into middle age, is still an immediate threat. Today's students are tomorrow's voters, and tomorrow's new voters are still at that age when they think themselves invincible, and disease and injury and death seem to be things that happen to other people. In states like Oregon, an initiative process frequently bypasses the legislative route of enacting many social policies. Already in Oregon and eleven other states, animal rights groups have moved from passing trapping and hunting laws— Oregon now bans leg-hold traps and hunting bears with dogs—to laws requiring teachers to provide and make known to parents alternatives to classroom dissection. It might not be long before they introduce initiatives banning the use of animals in the training of surgeons or defining cruelty to animals in a way that applies to researchers. Slanted "educational" materials and activities in our high schools today could have significant consequences in an election tomorrow. P*e*TA's crusade, even more than the children's crusade long ago, could well lead to large-scale tragedy.

WE GET LETTERS

We get two types of letters. One type, in the small minority, thanks us. Frequently, the authors are themselves seriously ill; more often, they are parents of a sick child.

More commonly, we get hate mail. Often these are not signed. Even if signed, as was a missive from Alicia Silverstone, they reflect an organized letter-writing campaign and little understanding of animal research. They have been prepared by one animal rights group or another, urging that they be sent to us, to our administrative leadership, and to state or federal elected representatives. Frequently cut and pasted from the Web site or Listserv that is sending out the directive, these letters come in waves of clones.

Often they are postcards that have been torn out of animal rights magazines. A few years ago during a six-week period, we received roughly five thousand identical, pre-printed postcards making outlandish claims about our activities. We say "roughly" because we found it more convenient to weigh them than count them.

The cloned cards mention the same canards—you can't extrapolate from animal studies to humans; cell culture techniques, computer simulations, and epidemiological studies make animal research unnecessary; research animals are stolen pets that are treated with criminal cruelty (See Appendix A). We don't know what the strategy is here. Perhaps it is a low-tech tactic akin to the electronic civil disobedience already described in Chapter 2, animal extremists hoping to bring a halt to animal cruelty under the weight of tons of mail. Possibly the cards do no more than give people who don't understand the situation well but think we are doing something wrong a simple way to do something right and good.

Among the hate mail, occasionally, we find original letters. Often these letters are disguised. Some authors pretend to be fifteen years old, yet speak with the verbal skills of someone much older. Inevitably they address how much the author cares about animals, perhaps meaning to suggest by inference that we do not.

Frequently, they reference Web sites of contrived images or allegations refuted long ago. The writers accept the images and allegations at face value. Of course, they could spend a little time on the Internet reading news stories confirming that independent investigations have found the claims to be without merit, but taking such time and care is not necessary if one's mind is already made up.

Sprinkled through most all the letters is the question, "How can you . . . ?" followed by some allegation of outlandish torture that would mark us criminals in the first degree. They discuss our work with a vigorous if limited vocabulary: valueless, frightful, atrocious, horrific, appalling, sickening, sadistic. In addition to vocabulary, block-letter handwriting, obscene expressions, including the F word, and sentiments that stop just short of illegal threats help set the tone. Often a correspondent has told us that he or she hopes our end is painful or that he or she won't see us "on the other side" because we deserve eternal damnation.

We have responded to every original letter, except those from writers who hide their identities and addresses. Every once in a while we see the value of this effort. A carefully and accurately worded response, challenging the erroneous beliefs and suggesting documented truth, will result in a grateful response that begins: "I had no idea. . . . " Occasionally people reveal that they were shocked just to get a response.

One of our favorite letters suggested, *"The effect of what you do should come back on your children."* Actually, that would be a good thing!

THE PRICE IS RIGHT

Cynics tell us that there is a second Golden Rule: "If you have the gold—YOU rule!" It applies, we think, in many of the nation's law schools. Many "follow the ice-cream truck" and develop programs that, to some measure, are governed by what benefactors are willing to support. This cynical version of the Golden Rule explains the development of animal law as a fast-growing specialty.

Which brings us to Bob Barker. Yes, the same Bob Barker who has cheerfully greeted eager consumers with "Come on down!" as the host for nearly thirty-five years of *The Price Is Right* television show and before that of *Truth or Consequences.* He has been a philanthropic supporter of animal law ever since the death of his wife in 1981. It is believed that she and his mother both influenced his concern, and in their names he has created a foundation. His generosity began with a one-million-dollar gift from FemantleMedia, the production company of *The Price Is Right,* to endow a chair of animal law at Harvard Law School. Barker's foundation then made one-million-dollar gifts to Northwestern University, the University of California at Los Angeles, Duke University, Stanford University, and Columbia University. He clearly is dedicated to this cause. He puts his mouth where his money is: "Animals need all the protection we can give them. We intend to train a growing number of law students in this area of the law in the hope that they will ultimately lead a national effort to make it illegal to brutalize and exploit these helpless creatures" (ABC).

Wait a minute . . . who is he talking about? Could he be suggesting that biomedical researchers brutalize and exploit helpless creatures?

Barker has the courage of his convictions. He is a vegetarian who does not wear leather and opposes the use of animals in entertainment. He concludes every program with a plea to spay and neuter pets, believing, as we do, that pet overpopulation is a serious problem. In this view he has faced the ire of some animal rightists who argue that spaying and neutering violate the "reproductive freedom" of animals—whatever that means. He has even forced a standoff with the producers of the Miss Universe Pageant over the use of fur coats on the show.

So, what about biomedical research? "I'm well aware of the cruelties and the mistreatment of animals in animal research," he announced, as he made his gift to Northwestern University. He then confessed that he had to "bite his lip and turn a blind eye" to the animal research going on at the university. In other words, in our imperfect world there is no such thing as a clean nickel. A contribution to a university conducting animal research may be abetting evildoers, but even so, Barker argues, "Many good things will come . . . students, [who] will go on to be lawyers, judges and even politicians who will write tougher laws" (Newbart).

If good comes from bad, it won't be for the first time in Barker's life. The inconvenient truth is that some years ago he was hospitalized and underwent surgery at George Washington University to remove a blockage in his left carotid artery (CBS [1]). If unattended, that blockage might have led to a stroke. Fortunately for animal rights fundraising, Barker survived his medical crisis to continue his philanthropic work at Northwestern and other universities, thanks in good part to surgical techniques perfected in animal models.

We are pleased that the dean of the Northwestern Law School, David Van Zandt, took an interpretation of the concept of animal law that is broader than that of securing animal rights. "Legal issues," he pointed out, "can cover a wide spectrum, ranging from patent and intellectual property law to criminal prosecution or defense, or constitutional law. Experimental animal cloning is a recent example of an intellectual property context where animal law issues have emerged" (*Northwestern Observer Online*).

What will be the topics of student education in Animal Law School? One likely issue will be the emerging debate about whether pets are properly considered to be property. The law already recognizes that animals are a special type of property. While discarding your baseball in the dumpster is not a crime, discarding your cat in the same dumpster is. The legal system contains anti-animal cruelty laws recognizing that we have special obligations and responsibilities to animals. Our ability to take responsibility, which distinguishes us from the rest of the animal pack, requires us to provide food and water, comfort, medical attention, and personal attention and interaction for our pets. These laws don't provide rights for animals, but they do establish penalties for cruel or negligent treatment by humans. The Animal Welfare Act establishes the basis of the federal legal bite for inhumane treatment of animals.

But here is where things become complex. Consider a case reported in *USA Today*. A patient underwent dental surgery, suffered unexpected adverse complications, and died. Family members filed suit against the doctor for negligence and sought hundreds of thousands of dollars of compensation for emotional distress. The patient was a sheepdog (Parker).

What is the economic value of that loss? Is it the fair market value of the property—that is, the dog named Lucky—at the time of the loss? Or did Lucky have additional value because it was a living creature? To the second question, many reasonable people will say "yes." Because Lucky had special value for having been loved a great deal, the family should be able to collect for emotional loss. No doubt the family can collect on the surgical bill and on the value of the animal at the time of loss—after all, they paid for services and have been denied the use of their property—but, because they lack standing, they might not win a hearing for their claim to be compensated for emotional injury.

"Standing" refers to the ability of a party to demonstrate that it has a connection to and would be harmed by a particular action. In the United States, you cannot sue unless you have been harmed. Animals are considered "chattel," or personal property. You can "own" an animal just as you can own a baseball. You can likewise sue to recover for damages inflicted to your property. But, as far as we know, no U.S. jurisdiction allows you to recover for harm—your pain and suffering— incurred in damage to your property. It is possible that an inventive attorney might develop a case for your recovery of the diminution in value of your pet caused by its pain or injury. Still, the top value is likely to be the value of the animal as property.

Some courts, recognizing that many animals have a special place in our world, have begun to move beyond the notion of animal as nothing but property. Since 1997, courts in Kentucky and California have awarded damages to pet owners for loss of companionship, emotional distress, and other factors that go beyond an animal's market value. These changes have the American Veterinary Medical Association (AVMA) likely casting an eye on the growing settlements in human medical malpractice cases, sniffing a potential problem. Recalling that it promotes the optimal health and well-being of animals and recognizes the role of responsible owners in providing for their animals' care, the AVMA argues, "Any change in terminology describing the relationship between animals and owners does not strengthen this relationship and may, in fact, diminish it. Such changes in terminology may decrease the ability of veterinarians to provide services and, ultimately, result in animal-suffering" (JAVMA). The Pennsylvania Veterinary Medical Association echoes that view, but with the additional argument that "loss of companionship—a measure of damages arising out of marital and parental relationships— should not be recoverable in litigation involving animals, particularly when it is not available for the loss of close family relatives" (Finkelstein).

Whatever we think of that issue, animal rightists take yet another step. They note that you do not have standing on behalf of the dog for its injuries. If you were to sue for additional compensation because poor veterinary treatment resulted in pain and suffering for the dog, the court would probably dismiss your suit without considering its merits.

So it was that one attorney at the 2006 Animal Rights Convention, after reminding partisans of this fact and after complaining that the only recourse, government entities that can prosecute for violations of animal protection laws, hadn't worked, argued for expanding the notion of standing. Observing that nothing in the Constitution prohibits suing on behalf of animals, Anuj Shah recommended introducing legislation explicitly granting individuals a right of action on behalf of animals when those individuals suffer (1) informational injury, or harm from the absence of information such as that required of research labs by the Animal Welfare Act, or (2) aesthetic injury, or harm caused by witnessing the mistreatment of animals (National Association for Biomedical Research).

Step by step, some animal law "reformers" advance still further. They propose considering animals as legal persons, thus removing a distinction between humans and animals that has been drawn by every culture. Anticruelty laws, which have been on the books for a long time and in a majority of states make animal abuse the felony it should be, are not enough. Animals must have legal rights, exercised for them by guardians.

There is a new word—guardian. Suddenly and with some shock we see the reason for the interest of proponents of animal legal rights in changing the words "pet owner" to "animal guardian." "Owners" implies that animals are but property; "guardians" suggests that they can have rights.

Not a few municipal jurisdictions have gone along with the word change, executing a find (owner) and replace (guardian) operation with electronic copies of their ordinances. West Hollywood, San Francisco, and Berkeley, California, and Boulder, Colorado have led the way. Amherst, Massachusetts; St. Louis, Missouri; Albany, New York; Windsor and Wanaque, New Jersey; Menomonee Falls, Wisconsin; Sherwood, Arizona; twenty-nine cities in California; and the entire state of Rhode Island have followed. It's probably coming to a city council near you soon.

We wonder if officials in these jurisdictions thought through all the implications of their verbal surgery. One who has thought about them is Charlotte Lacroix. This veterinarian and lawyer raises the following questions:

- Can guardians treat their own pets?
- Can pets make demands of their guardians?
- Can pets sue their guardians? Veterinarians? Government?
- Can guardians be divested of their property rights?
- Who will pay and provide for care of divested pets?
- Who is responsible for veterinary bills, if care that benefits the pet was not approved by the guardian?
- What do shelters do with abandoned animals?
- What if a veterinarian disagrees with the guardian?

Dr. Lacroix's comments on this set of questions merits quoting in full:

> There's no question in my mind that animals are not cars, but there's also no question in my mind that animals are not necessarily akin to children. They don't have the same needs, the same interests, nor are they humans with the same roles in society, etc. Are we going to make them children overnight just by changing terminology, or instead maybe continue to strengthen the animal cruelty statutes by imposing additional obligations on pet owners and enforcing such laws before proposing new legal paradigms? Can we chip away at this property concept so that we recognize animals are not cars, but on the other hand, not turn the law on its head to take animals from property status to basically human status without debating in an open forum on which specific legal "rights" animals should and should not be conferred? (Finkelstein)

Calling pet owners pet guardians and recognizing legal rights for animals could result in a paradoxical end: the end altogether of companion animals. Once rights are recognized, would not owning, selling, and breeding animals be tantamount to their enslavement? If animals are deemed legal persons and people can file suits on their behalf, can't your neighbor sue for the long hours your riding horse has to put in "against its will"?

Nevertheless, Eliot Katz, president of IDA and current supervisor of Matt Rossell, believes word change is crucial to "elevating" the public's perception of animals. He observes, correctly, that action follows language, and that therefore changing terminology and thinking of the animal/human relationship differently is "terribly important because it's a major step in ending a great deal of animal pain and suffering" (Allan). According to Katz, the shift away from seeing an animal as an owned thing is similar to the shift that gradually gave women and African Americans status as citizens, rather than property to be used according to the arbitrary will of a husband or "master."

Thirteen states (Arizona, Connecticut, Florida, Massachusetts, Michigan, Minnesota, Missouri, New Jersey, New York, Oregon, Pennsylvania, Texas, Washington) and the District of Columbia have animal law sections or committees, and fifty law schools offer, or plan to offer, animal law courses, reading groups, and/or seminars. These committees, courses, and seminars will be important in determining how much of the animal rights agenda is implemented. They will, however, follow public sentiment. It is our fear that an uneducated or inattentive public could allow the agenda to go forward thoughtlessly, not suspecting its negative effect on animal research and its threat to all the good that comes from biomedical research.

An ethicist and lawyer, Jerrold Tannenbaum, speaking at ONPRC, sketched that scenario. Animals become "persons." A researcher is sued by a chimpanzee for false imprisonment, slavery, and deprivation of its freedom. The plaintiff, in a surprise move, calls the chimp, which now will maintain it is a person with rights, to the stand. The chimp, taught a sign language routine, describes its cage and its desire to be set free (Tannenbaum).

The case goes to the jury.

HITCHING A RIDE: THE ANIMAL RIGHTS MOVEMENT AND ENVIRONMENTALISM

Releasing captive animals into the environment is a victory for the animals and for the environment, right? Not exactly. A

1997 mink farm raid in Oregon resulted in most of the "liberated" mink dying in the raid's aftermath (lacking survival skills, they often succumb to thirst or starvation or a car, the rumbling noise of which they mistake for a food cart).

Besides that, not all environmentalists agree that the causes of animal liberation and environmentalism are the same thing. Nevertheless, another strategy of the animal rights movement is to hitch a ride with the environmental movement. Among organizations that are not pleased to have animal rightists as fellow travelers is The Nature Conservancy (TNC). One of its concerns is the ecological devastation being wreaked by wild boars in Hawaii. Brought by nineteenth-century traders, these boars now constitute the single greatest threat to the islands' rain forests and rare wildlife. According to TNC official Ron Geatz, one boar weighing as much as three hundred pounds can destroy a thousand square feet of rain forest a day. Half of Hawaii's unique forests, which are home to thousands of species found nowhere else on Earth, have been lost already. Soil erosion caused by the deforestation has also contaminated watersheds and silted coral reefs.

In 1994, TNC was employing several methods of protecting the environment—fencing, live cage trapping, hunting, and, in locations of extreme isolation and rugged terrain, setting lethal snare traps for the pigs. Then P*e*TA co-founder Alex Pacheco visited Molokai and Maui. An advertising blitz followed. A full-page newspaper ad displaying a photograph of the daughter of a P*e*TA employee holding a kid goat screamed, "The Nature Conservancy Kills Kids." With that came a plea asking for money to stop the killing of baby goats, wild pigs, and other free-roaming animals in Hawaii (*Washington City Paper*).

Similar stories abound, stories about goats on the Galapagos Islands, red foxes in southern California, mountain goats on Washington's Olympic peninsula, zebra mussels in the Great Lakes, rabbits in Australia. Humans introduce an invasive species to an environment where the species has no predators. When the newcomers push native species to the brink of extinction, environmentalists move in for the rescue, only to find animal rightists blocking their way.

Human folly isn't limited to introducing invasive species into an ecosystem. We also overhunt and then overprotect various species. In Michigan, Native Americans once played an important role in stabilizing the population of beavers, which they trapped for pelts used in clothing and shelter. Then, in the nineteenth century, white trappers nearly wiped out the population as they attempted to satisfy a worldwide craze for felt hats manufactured from the pelts. Today, with the disappearance of both Native American and white trappers, quite the opposite problem has emerged. Industrious beavers, unchecked by trappers, have built dams all over the upper Midwest. The dams, by turning trout streams into strings of tiny lakes, are threatening a delicate ecological balance. But can environmentalists restore the wise management practices of Native Americans? Not if animal rightists have their way and succeed in disrupting species restoration efforts.

That's what happened when researchers at the University of California at Irvine were attempting to bring a flock of California condors back from near extinction. Part of their patient endeavor was to use turkey vultures to trace the effects of dioxins, one of the suspects in the mystery of the disappearing condors. Their research was halted when members of the ALF "liberated" the vultures.

The problem with the animal rights agenda, of course, is the priority it gives to individual animals, rather than the whole environment. P*e*TA leader Newkirk envisions a world where, "when two animals fight, human beings will intervene" (McCabe, 190). Environmentalists might be amused by her vision if it didn't have such destructive consequences. They know that exclusive care for individuals can entail the decline of a species and have drastic consequences for a whole ecosystem.

Consider the white-tailed deer in Michigan's Great Swamp National Wildlife Refuge. For some years before 1974, while hunting was banned, these deer showed signs of stress caused by overpopulation. Even though scarce forage kept their number stable, many adult males appeared stunted and carried only spikes or the four-point antlers characteristic of two-year-olds. Beginning in 1974, hunters were allowed to cull about one-fifth of the population each fall. Having more food over the winter, the remaining deer grew larger, stronger, and healthier, and each spring they replenished their number (Woolf).

The attachment of many animal rightists to individual animals rather than to species makes us wonder if the movement is based in reality. Nature's primary "interest" is in the success of species. Individuals, despite the value that some of them have for passing on their genes and all of them have as food for predators, are secondary and replaceable.

Like all animals, we humans act in self-preservation. With the tool for evolutionary success peculiar to us—our remarkable intelligence—we have developed technologies of production and information that have extended our lives and improved our well-being. We have nurtured impulses toward generosity and constructed moral and legal codes that have united us against a hostile world. We have used our intelligence to gain an upper hand even on disease-causing viruses and bacteria that are our most challenging predators.

Until quite recently in history, these triumphs helped maintain ecological balance. Now, success itself threatens to become our undoing. The unintended result of spectacular advances in food production and health care have contributed to a population explosion that puts all life on Earth, including our own, at risk. We have thrown nature so off balance that our continued self-existence now depends on learning how to preserve other species, both plants and animals. Our instrument for saving arable land, rain forests, the ozone layer, and salmon runs, however, is the very brain that has brought us to crisis. The only useful prescription for our ills is intelligent rather than sentimental thinking.

This brings us back to the story of P*e*TA and TNC. Add another character to the story—Bonnie Dunbar, PhD, professor of cellular biology at Baylor College of Medicine. Dunbar was the first to demonstrate that elephants in the wild can be sterilized through immunization. Using proteins taken from the ovum's *zona pellucida* (a mesh-like casing that controls the access of sperm to an egg), Dunbar trains immune-system antibodies to recognize and destroy the receptors on an egg's surface that are required for sperm penetration. This strategy, which requires no more than one inoculation delivered by dart gun, could be a practical means of stabilizing populations of free-roaming animal populations (Crawley).

There are several reasons that this and other developments in contraceptive research intrigue conservationists. It is crucial for the future of endangered species that we learn how to stabilize populations of their predators and improve their gene pools. A practical method of contraception for wild animals would allow TNC to someday bring the population of Hawaiian boars under control without using painful and lethal snare traps. Such a contraceptive strategy could also be used to shrink populations of endangered species such as the elephants in Africa, a counterintuitive strategy for invigorating the herd and favoring its survival. Finally, an efficient contraceptive strategy promises to alleviate the main problem for all species—human overpopulation.

Even animal rightists became interested in Dunbar's research. It put them, however, in a quandary: Dunbar's investigations are conducted with laboratory animals and depend on decades of animal research by other scientists. Animal rightists, evidently, aren't eager to admit that animal research can be the source of potential cures for the environment.

Although not all environmentalists enjoy having animal rightists as fellow travelers, there are some who do. These are the "deep ecologists" who tell us that we humans have an obligation to recognize ourselves as existing *within* rather than *above* nature. We are parts of a macro-organism structured much like a microcosmic cell, and we must relate to land, plants, and animals as to other parts of that same and greater whole. According to sociobiologist E. O. Wilson, the direction of our responsibility must be focused outward toward all of nature—ecocentric—rather than inward on our own species—anthropocentric (Wilson).

An insightful critic of deep ecology is Boris Zeide. He draws attention to the main error of the view of nature as a macro-organism—"its blindness to what Darwin called the struggle for life" (Zeide, 976). Nature is an environment of individuals and species, not an integrated organism. Individuals and species are not subject to any central control, as are the molecular and cellular units of individual plants or animals. They compete against each other in the struggle to survive, so that the notion of health applies to them as individuals and species but not to nature as a whole. In fact, the health of one individual or species may entail the misery and death of another. Finally, individuals and species can be both beneficial and harmful—we preserve some mosquito populations for their usefulness to amphibians and fish, but control other populations for the sake of human health.

Zeide's points seem both on the mark and obvious. Still, deep ecologists exert a strong appeal in today's world. Is that appeal due simply to ignorance, as if deep ecologists and their animal rights allies simply skipped their college course on Darwin and have made all their forays into nature in a recreational vehicle? Stephen Budiansky thinks not: Something more powerful even than ignorance is at the root of their peculiar view of nature. That something is myth (Budiansky [1], 127–52).

Animal rightists and deep ecologists, according to Budiansky, subscribe to the myth of an original nature, perfect and peaceful, that has been spoiled by human doing. Nature can be vigorous and beautiful if only humans live and let live within it, rather than use it and attempt to tend to its care. And we *can* live and let live in the garden because that, in fact, is what our ancestors did in the "good old days" before the industrial and technological revolutions.

You may recognize this myth as a secular version of the Biblical myth of Eden, the garden cursed by the folly of human sin. Notice, however, this significant difference: while the Biblical paradise was lost in mythic time, nature as imagined by animal rightists has been spoiled within human history and, in fact, during modern times. Placing the myth in history, deep ecologists give it a powerful punch line: we can and must return to Eden by recapturing the way of life of our ancestors, noble savages.

The problem, however, is that there never have been any noble savages. Primitive peoples laid waste to their landscape and sometimes drove species to extinction just as surely, if not on as large a scale, as their modern descendants. Never mind that. "With Eden established as the reference point for nature and the noble savage the standard for human conduct," Budiansky notes, deep ecologists and animal rightists "have a fairly easy job of horrifying the rest of us with tales of human actions that appear to depart from these totally artificial norms" (Budiansky [1], 130).

There is a cruel irony hidden in the live-and-let-live ethic of deep ecology. The less we depend on domesticated and individual animals for food and clothing, the more likely we are to endanger the survival of various species. Our primitive ancestors lived in direct and total dependence upon animals; they made their dwellings, covered their bodies, and carried their water with animal hides. We, on the other hand, construct dwellings of wood and steel and glass, fabricate our clothes of synthetics, and carry our water in PVC pipes and plastic bottles. In the process, we destroy forests, degrade the soil, and pollute the air and the water that are habitat for wildlife. We introduce chemicals and hormones into the food chain that disrupt the development and functioning of the reproductive systems of hundreds of species. The vinyl shoes and fake furs preferred by animal rightists take their toll, if not on individual animals, then certainly on the environment.

Environmental philosopher William Cronon goes to the heart of the secular myth of the garden and finds that in the myth humans are not so much within the environment as actually entirely outside the sphere of the natural:

> If we allow ourselves to believe that nature, to be true, must also be wild, then our very presence in nature represents its fall. The place where we are is the place where nature is not. If this is so—if by definition wilderness leaves no place for human beings, save perhaps as contemplative sojourners enjoying

their leisurely reverie in God's natural cathedral—then also by definition it can offer no solution to the environmental and other problems that confront us. (Cronon, 80–81)

Here is a surprising twist. Deep ecologists and hitchhiking animal rightists profess to relocate the human species within nature. In fact, however, like the angels who barred the gates of Eden after Adam and Eve's transgression, they would save nature by keeping the human species out. Cronon draws the absurd conclusion: "If nature dies because we enter it, then the only way to save nature is to kill ourselves" (Cronon, 83).

Absurd as it is, P*e*TA's Newkirk has drawn just this conclusion:

> I am not a morose person, but I would rather not be here.
> I don't have any reverence for life, only for the entities themselves.
> I would rather see a blank space where I am.
> This will sound like fruitcake stuff again,
> but at least I wouldn't be harming anything. (Brown, B10)

With Cronon we have to acknowledge that humans, for good or ill, are inextricably part of nature. If we stand outside of nature in any way at all, it is not, as deep ecologists and animal rightists would argue, because we alone are obliged to forgo action aimed at our own survival. Rather, it is because, with the tools of our evolutionary success—intelligence and conscience—we alone can and must take responsibility for nature.

The truth is that the doctrine of animal rights either undermines our necessary and urgent commitment to the environment or, in the case of its alliance with deep ecology, leads to absurdity. Don't count on that truth to blunt efforts of the animal rightists to identify their cause with environmentalism. Alignment of the two movements serves the animal movement too well. A few years ago, one of the editors of *Animals' Agenda* left that publication for *E* magazine. Animal liberation, he announced, is still controversial, but concern for the environment is respectable (Knox, 35). He was candid about the direction that the animal rights movement should go: it should target mainstreamers like you and me who care about marshlands and flyways, ancient forests and salmon runs. What could be more "natural" than for us to be open to animal rights?

Chapter 5

War Casualties

Intimidation is a little like pornography. It is hard to define, but you know it when you see it.

Craig Rosebraugh's unknown "elves" may have intimidated mink farmers, but they have done little to advance his revolution. More focused intimidation, however, abetted by traditional methods of writing letters and lobbying congress, has brought about at least two stunning victories for animal extremists. The victories are a serious threat to the whole enterprise of biomedical research.

The Cases of Michael Podell, DVM and Dario Ringach, PhD

Michael Podell was an associate professor in the Department of Veterinary Clinical Sciences and Center for Retrovirus Research, College of Veterinary Medicine, at Ohio State University. He was also director of the Comparative Neurology Service. He investigated how the AIDS virus enters the brain and how the resulting infection can be recognized in its earliest stages. He also studied new forms of epilepsy treatment in dogs and screened a number of potential drugs for their neurotoxic effects. In just a few words, Podell developed animal models of human and animal disease.

If you are going to study a human disease you can't, for ethical reasons, perform the initial work in humans; you have to develop a model. Some models may be *in vitro*—literally, in glass tubes—but as you learn more and more, you must eventually test ideas *in vivo*—in living animals. That means you have to have a way of producing the disease that allows you to study it.

Let's consider AIDS, one of Podell's interests. You could take its causative agent, the human immunodeficiency virus (HIV), grow it in a test tube, and kill it by pouring bleach on it. Do you now have a way to kill HIV? Yes, you do. Do you have a treatment that can be used in humans? Absolutely not: bleach is toxic. Killing HIV in a test tube and killing it in a living animal are two very different accomplishments.

To complicate things further, viruses grow differently in test tubes than in humans. Humans have an immune system: test tubes do not. A virus growing in a test tube is not a good model for the human disease, but drugs that don't kill the test tube virus probably won't work in humans either—and these might be eliminated from further consideration.

Animal models allow closer approximation to a human response. They are not perfect, of course; animals host different diseases and different responses. While the fundamentals of life are the same—there is a 67 percent similarity between the DNA of humans and earthworms—there are differences in species and even in individual animals. Some animals are good human-like models for one thing and some for another; some have a cardiovascular system that is similar to humans while others have similar skin.

Let's now imagine that we discover a treatment for AIDS that works in animals. Does it also work in humans? The answer is "maybe." The answer might be "yes" because basic metabolic processes are similar in animals and humans; it might be "no" because some processes are not identical, causing some drugs to be metabolized differently in humans and animals. This is true even within a species of animal. It is known, for example, that collies metabolize some drugs differently than beagles and that drugs that work for beagles cannot be used for collies. Drugs that kill some species have little effect in others, a fact that allows us to create a pill that kills worms in pets, yet does no harm to dogs or cats.

Drug testing, which begins in cell cultures, eventually involves human beings. Much of our drug development data has been obtained from white, male adults. Caucasians are chosen because the U.S. population is predominantly Caucasian; males because they are sometimes easier to study than females because they lack the added hormonal complexity of a menstrual cycle; adults because they are capable of consent and cooperation. We now know that different sexes, races, and ages all metabolize drugs differently. Data obtained from white adult males are not universally applicable, and individual differences explain why people react differently to the same drugs, why some people are allergic to certain drugs and others are not.

Scientists approach these complexities by screening drugs with disease-causing virus or bacteria in test tubes. Then they move on to rodents and, in some cases and in smaller numbers, to monkeys. This animal testing provides leads, and although it is true that it can yield false positives and false negatives, it is unquestionably valuable. Finally, researchers move on to clinical trials in human volunteers. Think of this as a pyramid, with *all* human beings just below the top. YOU are at the very top, because no one knows how you will respond to a drug that works for others. There is one last problem: YOU are very different in your response at age two, twenty, or eighty. The YOU of yesterday responds differently to drugs than the YOU of tomorrow.

Podell was working at the animal interface to human disease, and although we never met him personally, we believe that he was quite good at what he did. We reach this conclusion because he was successful at obtaining NIH grants, a rigorous process involving expert review and funding of only the very best. He also published, regularly, in peer-reviewed journals, a standard of quality indicating that he was able to produce valuable data that could be used to develop therapeutic approaches in humans. He would not design drugs—generally, pharmaceutical companies do that—but would discover information and identify approaches that could guide their design. Podell received a BA degree from the University of North Carolina and did graduate work in Israel at Tel Aviv University. He then received a veterinary degree from Tufts University and conducted an internship in New York. He was a diplomate of the American College of Veterinary Internal Medicine in Neurology.

His work soon attracted the ire of animal extremists. Few of them, if any, were in a position to understand the importance of his work and the extent of its oversight, or to know that the NIH review committee ranked his research among the most valuable in the country. All they knew is that he used kittens.

Podell came under attack. He began to receive threatening calls. The university was inundated with chain emails (Stolberg). With the mutations inherent in chain emails—think of children who whisper a story to each other that gets more detailed and more skewed with each repetition—the purpose of his work, the number of animals, and the benefits became blurred as the months passed. Like all email chains, those attacking him seldom got updated with current information. Their correspondence grew in viciousness.

In addition to receiving emails and anonymous phone calls, including death threats, Podell saw his studies become the target of lawsuits (Stolberg). A Columbus, Ohio, group, Protect Our Earth's Treasures, began demonstrations and a letter-writing campaign hoping to block federal approval of his research. Mercy for Animals weighed in with a pejorative summary that included no mention of his purposes, methods, or results:

> To conduct this research, Dr. Podell will subject cats to spinal taps and other painful procedures before killing them to examine their brains. These procedures will likely cause extreme pain, distress, and suffering for the cats. In order to conduct this research, the National Institute of Drug Abuse (NIDA), a division of the National Institutes of Health (NIH), has so far funded Dr. Podell's experiment with $700,000. In order to

complete this study, Dr. Podell will receive $1.68 million over five years. (Mercy for Animals)

According to Neal Barnard, MD, of PCRM, research into the effects of amphetamines and HIV is more properly done in HIV-positive individuals already being treated with amphetamines for depression and in HIV-positive drug abusers. Dr. Barnard stated: "Cats cannot show language deficits, subtle learning problems, hallucinations, delusions, or other neurological effects that are known to occur in drug abusers." He added that "the cat virus FIV is very different from HIV, and cat results would not apply to people" (Barnard).

Researchers would have taken notice if such a dogmatic assertion had come from an expert on AIDS. But not even Barnard, a psychiatrist by training, portrays himself as such. Barnard and PCRM prepared a lawsuit against NIH under the Freedom of Information Act for withholding details about Podell's work (PCRM).

In June 2002, Podell published a significant study related to his feline AIDS research. His findings offered important clues about pathways and mechanisms that might explain why drug abuse quickens the rate of AIDS infection and AIDS-related dementia. A little more than a week later, Ohio State announced that Podell was leaving the university, and Podell confirmed that after having several death threats, he had accepted an opportunity elsewhere. He had been scared off in a matter of only months (Stolberg).

Podell also revealed that his departure was due, in part, to the fact that he never received the support he needed from the university in dealing with animal rights activists. In fact, in an email to a Columbus newspaper he indicated that lack of support from his university was the main reason for his exit. Dr. Podell wrote, "The Ohio State University could not provide an environment conducive to continuation of my research or my role as a clinician and instructor. There were many opportunities for these problems to be addressed appropriately, but an insufficient response pattern was taken by the administration here" (Caton). OSU public relations officer Earle Holland appeared to confirm Podell's view. He told the *Other Paper*, "Mike [Podell] would like to have a definitive statement out of the institution [supporting him and condemning the animal rights protesters] to put a stop to this. That's not something an institution can do" (Caton).

So OSU was left without Podell but with a $1.68 million grant from the federal government. (For reasons of compliance and responsibility, the federal government always awards grants to institutions, not individuals, even though it is common for researchers to identify grants that came from their initiative as "theirs.") Grantees can request that grants move from one institution to another, but Podell did not make this request. In October 2002, it was announced that two of Podell's former assistants would take over the project.

Two days after the announcement of Podell's departure, OSU president William E. Kirwan defended the university and explained the necessary and humane use of laboratory animals in biomedical research:

> [O]ur researchers will continue to be diligent stewards of the animals in their care, and the university will continue to be committed to maintaining the high standards that we have demonstrated.
>
> We all owe a great deal to researcher Michael Podell and his colleagues for conducting such research while being impeded relentlessly by activists opposed to using animals in research. He and his family have received repeated threats by email and telephone.
>
> Yet, it is thanks to their great courage and tenacity that we now better understand the threat viruses of this [HIV] type pose to human health. (Kirwan)

A USDA inspection gave Dr. Podell and OSU a clean bill of health regarding all aspects of the research and animal care programs.

At the time of Podell's resignation, Frankie L. Trull, president of the Foundation for Biomedical Research, the nation's oldest and largest organization devoted to promoting public understanding, respect, and support for humane and responsible research, wrote an open letter to Elias Zerhouni, MD, head of the NIH, and sent copies to the acting director of the National Institute on Drug Abuse, the Secretary of Health and Human Services and the Ohio Congressional Delegation.

> We are deeply concerned about the recent decision by Dr. Michael Podell to discontinue his NIH-funded research at Ohio State University. It is well known that this critical study of the effect of methamphetamine drugs on HIV-infected people has been subject to a steady and often violent campaign of harassment against Dr. Podell, his family, and Ohio State University veterinary school since the NIH grant was announced in October 2000.
>
> We are alarmed that a small, vocal, and often violent segment of the animal rights movement, rather than the scientific research community, is increasingly being allowed to define the parameters of medical research expertise. Too much is at stake to allow this to continue. We fear that the loss of Dr. Podell and his research project is merely the beginning of an ever-escalating campaign against research discovery and medical advancement.
>
> On behalf of FBR's broad-based scientific constituency, we urge you to provide the leadership necessary to protect biomedical research, educate the public and decision-makers of its value to all Americans, and counter the inaccurate claims and destructive tactics of the animal rights movement. (Foundation Biomedical Research [2])

Podell is now engaged in the practice of veterinary medicine. As we were completing this book, we located him. In a written message from the Primate Center email address, we told him that we wanted to talk about this part of his life, although we didn't specifically mention our preparation of this book. We told him that, if he didn't answer, we would respect his privacy and not contact him again. We have respected that commitment.

We wouldn't want to leave you with the impression that Podell's departure from animal research was unique. In August 2006, a vision researcher at UCLA, Dario Ringach, PhD, sent a message to the ALF pledging to cease his neurological experiments with macaque monkeys. The email message was to the point, "You win," it began, according to ALF's press office. He asked that his name be removed from Web sites exposing his "atrocities," and "that [his] family be left alone"[1] (*Inside Higher Ed*).

The Web sites that concerned him had posted his picture, home address, phone number, lab address, lab phone number, email, and other contact information (Primate Freedom). Demonstrators had conducted protests at his home and distributed leaflets about his research to neighbors (Mitchell [2]). Just a month earlier the Stop Huntington Animal Cruelty (SHAC) Web site contained the information that Ringach was "a demented and deranged experimenter who paralyzes monkeys for 120 hours, embeds coils in their eyes, tracks their gaze, and finally slaughters them" (SHAC [2]).

Ringach, whose work has been funded by a ten-year grant—ordinarily, grants extend for three years; a ten-year grant is an award for very promising science—focuses on visual perception and neurophysiology. He is interested in cortical dynamics, circuitry, function, and mathematical modeling of visual receptive fields—how the brain is "wired" for sight, how the brain interprets images, and how we compensate for changes in the field of vision while we are moving. Such information is helpful for understanding how people recover from visual problems after strokes.

We can imagine the nature and depth of Ringach's concern. Earlier in the summer, activists claiming to be members of ALF took credit for leaving a "Molotov cocktail" at the home of another UCLA researcher, Lynn Fairbanks, whose research also involves monkeys (Jaschik). Apparently, however, the incendiary device was misdelivered, winding up on the doorstep of a seventy-year-old neighbor. Arson investigators reported that had the device detonated, the inhabitants would have had a very difficult time escaping their house, which backed up against a hillside.

UCLA's Media Relations Office promptly issued a response to the ALF announcement about Ringach: "UCLA strongly condemns this terrorist attack and deplores violence intended to injure people or damage property for any reason" (NBC4 TV). When Ringach, who is a sought-after speaker with an excellent track record of scientific contribution, decided to end his work in a successful research area, the same office issued another statement:

> The recent announcement by a UCLA professor that he has suspended research on primates illustrates the damage to society caused by the illegal terrorist activities of some animal rights groups. We all suffer when animal rights activists attempt to intimidate researchers by physically threatening and harassing them and their families, including young children.
>
> To be so extreme as to use violent tactics aimed at halting animal research is to take away hope from millions of people with cancer, AIDS, heart disease, and hundreds of other diseases.
>
> UCLA will continue to fulfill its commitment to improving human health and the quality of life through research that makes use of the most advanced scientific methods available, including humane, closely monitored, and legal animal research when necessary. (UCLA Office of Media Relations)

Frankie L. Trull, president of FBR, used the event to draw public attention to pending legislation aimed at protection of researchers:

> Congress is currently considering legislation to address, among other tactics, the intimidation and harassment of scientists and their families with the implication of doing physical harm. Congress must act swiftly to amend the Animal Enterprise Protection Act (HR 4239 and S 1926) in order to properly equip the FBI to investigate and prosecute animal extremists who are opposed to life-saving medical research. (FBR [3])

As a footnote to Ringach's request for mercy for his family in exchange for giving up a productive primate research career, Jean Barnes, director of the Primate Freedom Project—she calls herself "The Barnstormer"—said that she had informed Dr. Ringach that his name would remain on the site until he provides the group with a videotape declaring that he would no longer use any animal in any experiment and apologizes for the nonhuman pain and suffering he has caused (Henig). That's sympathy!

Clearly the cases of Podell and Ringach were wins for the animal extremists. Whether they are also wake-up calls for the rest of us remains to be seen.

A second, more hopeful footnote. In November 2006, law enforcement got the new tool urged by Trull when the Animal Enterprise Terrorism Act passed both houses and was signed into law by the President. This legislation prohibits "third-party targeting" of companies and employees that do business with animal enterprises (vendors, suppliers, banks, insurance companies of facilities and of the friends and family members of researchers). It also prohibits making veiled threats to individuals and their families and intentionally placing persons in reasonable fear of death or serious bodily injury because of their relationship with an animal enterprise. Those who violate this law face fines or jail terms ranging from one year to life for actions of harassment and intimidation, including damaging property, trespassing, and making threats. The law also provides for restitution of economic damages.

STUDENTS: DOCTORS-TO-BE MISSING IN ACTION?

Have animal extremists scared off any students who were considering careers in research or veterinary medicine? Unfortunately, we have very little good data to help answer this question. "Direct action"—bombings, personal harassment, and threats—has been occurring with regularity in the United States only during the last ten years, although somewhat longer in the UK. Attacks and the damages that result from them have been reported in the popular press only fairly recently, and only in the last few years have they become the topic of open discussion, even in the research and academic community. Their effects on students will probably not become apparent for several more years.

Also, it is hard to tease out the fear factor from other influences on the choice of research careers. It appears, for example, that possessing a PhD or an MD/PhD degree doesn't have the same attraction that it did in the 1950s and 1960s, when the Salk and Sabin vaccines were life-saving novelties for the general public and researchers enjoyed respect and even adulation. Then, too, it is not a secret that many well-educated and skilled medical researchers avoided military service in Vietnam by enlisting in the Public Health Service. The impetus that drove these brilliant and hard-working people into the intramural programs at the NIH, which flourished in part due to them, is now gone.

Even if we could find evidence that fewer of our most talented youth are going into research, the cause of that trend would not be clear. It is possible that today's research funding environment, in which young scientists find it much more difficult to win grants, has led them in the direction of more secure futures in business or law or medicine.

We do know, from The National Academies' Research Council report, *Critical Needs for Research in Veterinary Science*, that the nation faces a critical shortage of research veterinarians, especially those trained in veterinary pathology, lab animal science, and veterinary research. The report also documents the fact that fewer veterinarians are going into food agriculture and public health research.

The inability of the nation's twenty-eight veterinary colleges to graduate enough trained veterinary researchers will result in a shortfall of hundreds of such critical professionals as early as this year. The shortfall will occur, of course, just when the public's need for such personnel is greater than ever due to the emergence of avian flu, mad cow disease, and other contagious illnesses that move across international borders and have a devastating impact on both animal and human populations. It is at a time, too, when political terrorists may target the food supply. The report concludes, "There is an urgent need to provide adequate resources for investigators, training programs, and facilities involved in veterinary research to seize the opportunities to improve and safeguard human and animal health" (Committee on the National Needs).

Why are careers in veterinary research less attractive?

In January 1990, mail received at the University of Tennessee from animal rights extremists threatened to assassinate a veterinary dean within the following twelve months (U.S. Department of Justice [2]). You can imagine the shiver that ran down the spines of faculty and graduate students there and in veterinary schools around the country. One month later, Hyram Kitchen, DVM, dean of the Veterinary School of the University of Tennessee and expert on the nature of animal pain and distress, was shot and killed on his private farm (U.S. Department of Justice [2]). Despite the fact that the murder remains unsolved to this day, can we blame any research veterinarians who believe that their worst fears were realized—the killing of a human being for the sake of animal rights? Or could we blame any students who might have changed their career plans as they pondered Kitchen's fate?

It is obvious from this story that just as much of our information about student attitudes is anecdotal, coming as it does from discussions with colleagues and with students, our case for the detrimental effects of animal extremism is largely conjectural. Still, we are not the only ones to make the case. Colin Blakemore, now chief executive of Britain's prestigious Medical Research Council, has acknowledged, "In a way, terrorists are winning. Students are not choosing to come into the arena of science involving animal research. There's a withering of that branch of science" (Turville-Heitz, 32).

Blakemore speaks of terrorists from experience. In the late 1980s, he became a target while studying cats as a model for the human vision system. His three children have received kidnapping threats and bomb scares, and the family house has had to be fitted out with panic buttons, triple locks, and a safe room (McKie [1]).

In the fall of 2005, four animal rights activists, claiming an association with the Animal Liberation Front, broke into the University of Iowa's Spence Laboratories and Seashore Hall. Iowa City, home of the university, is nestled in Midwest farm country where farm animals have been a vital part of local history and the economy. It is hard to imagine a setting that could be more accepting of the humane use of rodents in research, their wild relatives being viewed as vermin by the farmers, who trap and kill them.

Nonetheless, the activists overturned equipment, poured acid on valuable data, and released more than three hundred mice and rats. They forced the closure of labs and offices for an average of six weeks and caused direct financial losses estimated at $450,000. They took time out to spray-paint "Science not Sadism" on the inner walls of the facility (Blumberg).

We can imagine the impact of all this on the graduate students, some of whom had to recreate materials and reproduce experiments and thus delay their graduation dates. It was clear from a security camera video and from a video made by the perpetrators themselves that the intruders had committed their act with anger and vengeance. We wonder whether the students whose work was destroyed considered other nonresearch options upon graduation.

After the event, the attackers sent emails to the press containing names, names of spouses, and home telephone numbers of the Psychology Department faculty, students, and graduate assistants taking part in research involving animals. They posted this information on Web sites in a presumptive effort to shame the investigators and attract others to torment them. "People here are still intimidated and frightened," said David Skorton, then president of the university and himself a former vice president of research at the same university (Dvorak).

"The financial aspect is the least of our problems," said Richard W. Bianco, vice president for research at the University of Minnesota, referring to an attack at that institution in 1999 that caused about two million dollars in damage. "The hardest thing is people see this and don't want to go into science. Why would they go into science when they can have their work threatened like that?" (Dvorak).

How can a university publish a four-color recruiting brochure featuring the picture of a smiling professional in a lab coat in light of the report of John Lewis, FBI deputy assistant director for counterterrorism, that in June 2005 the agency had 150 open investigations of arson, bombings, and other violence linked to animal rights and eco-terrorism? (Elias). Most students that we would want to apply to our research training programs are smart enough to know that one bomb can kill them and one attack in the lab can destroy a life's work.

Some researchers may take all this in stride, but graduate or even undergraduate students? We were taken aback by the directness and honesty in a note we found in an employment listing on a well-known researcher's Web site:

> [Y]ou should be aware that due to the highly controversial nature of this research . . . I have personally received many threatening messages, and one of my personal friends was a victim of the infamous Unabomber. Animal rights groups are also an issue. You must be prepared to deal with assaults from every quarter: skeptical colleagues, indifferent department chairs, hostile press and fringe individuals, politically hobbled funding agencies, and students who lack the skill and commitment to participate meaningfully in your research. My advice is: only press forward with this area of research as your chosen path if you can conceive of doing nothing other than this. . . . On the other hand, this is a really great area for research. (Dennis)

Care to apply?

CHAPTER 6

WAR CASUALTIES: ALL OF US

Marcia Bryan's daughter Stephanie has juvenile, or type-II, diabetes. So do, approximately, another three million children in the United States. What makes Stephanie remarkable is that, thanks to her mom, a nurse, she knows she is alive today because of animal research. Her house is something of a Noah's Ark, home to a cat named Al Capone, who was adopted from the pound; a dog named BJ; a parrot; two hamsters; and a tankful of hermit crabs. But this lover of animals appreciates most the pound dogs with which two Canadian doctors, Frederick Banting and Charles Best, conducted the experiments that led to the discovery of insulin almost a hundred years ago.

Although Stephanie is grateful for having insulin, she knows it is not a cure. Long-range statistics for children like her are grim. Shortened life expectancy, vision loss, kidney failure, and cardiovascular complications cloud her future. It is not surprising that Stephanie and her family track stories about current research. Every day they think, "This may be the day," when they hear of a breakthrough. "We are patient," Marcia says, "and get disappointed only when we wake up to read about a research laboratory being vandalized or an animal rights protest taking place at a research hospital."

Americans are keenly interested in their health and listen carefully for stories of advances in the treatment of diabetes and heart disease and cancer and arthritis and AIDS and all the diseases that afflict us. At the same time, we don't often make the connection that Marcia Bryan made for her daughter. This treatment and that medication and those wise words from the doctor—all of it, with the exception of the advice to get plenty of bed rest, come from animal research. That is something that many of us would rather not think about. We are not as disappointed as Stephanie or Marcia if we hear of animal rights attacks on animal research.

A World Without Animal Research

The fact is that it's hard for us today to imagine the world before biomedical research. Thanks to public health and hygiene movements (which received impetus from animal research proving the transmission of disease by germs), better diet, vaccines, insulin, antibiotics, and heart surgery:

- A baby girl born today in the United States can expect to live seventy-eight years; a century ago, the same child would have lived forty-four years on average.
- Death rates from influenza, which killed more people in 1919 than all the battles of World War I, are down over 85 percent.
- Tuberculosis rates are only 10 percent of what they were in the 1930s and 1940s, when sanitariums all over the world cared for thousands of patients, 50 percent of whom died.
- Diphtheria, smallpox, polio, syphilis, pertussis, and measles, which used to kill thousands, are now eliminated, over 90 percent reduced, or worrisome only as potential terrorist weapons.
- Measles, mumps, and rubella have been virtually eliminated in the United States. (Gilmartin, 1)

Indeed, as William Paton has reminded us, life and health were different "even as late as the 1930s, [when] a schoolboy could have lost a companion from tuberculosis, mastoid infection, diphtheria, or scarlet fever, and might play with a friend crippled by polio, [and when] deformity, pain, and disability were familiar experiences" (Paton, 2).

The current high tide of the animal rights movement—marked best, perhaps, by Germany's having included protection of animals as part of its Basic Law (Nature Neuroscience [1])—is coming in at the very time when animal research is most necessary and most promising. The sequencing of the human genome has set the stage for discovering the functions of genes, but functional genomics can proceed only with the use of animals that model the absence or the overexpression of genes of interest. The isolation of embryonic stem cells has opened up the possibility of stem cell therapy for conditions such as heart disease and diabetes, brain degeneration, and nervous system injury, but scientists require animals to learn how stem cells become heart tissue, pancreatic or brain cells and to test the efficacy of such cells in treatments that could be alternatives to tissue or whole-organ transplants. The emergence of viruses such as HIV, Ebola virus, West Nile virus, and hantavirus make animal models of the diseases they cause as critical as animal models were in the eradication of smallpox and polio. Biomedical research, which is possible because all species are variations and expansions on common themes in nature, seems more than ever an ethical imperative.

Will we understand how critical animal research is before it is too late? Not until Carl Sagan's doctors explained that the procedure of transplanting bone marrow they were prescribing for him was dependent on decades of basic research and preclinical (animal) testing did this well-known and respected science communicator change his criticism of animal research to a "conflicted" endorsement (Sagan, 20). Not until Christopher Reeve's physician told him that the only hope for spinal cord injury victims lies in animal studies did "Superman" change from opponent to spokesman for biomedical research. Few advocates or sympathizers with animal rights, when faced with illness and the possibility of death, refuse medical treatments that come from animal research. When they are suffering, it would be mean-spirited to hold them to the harsh demands of ethical consistency, but we could wish that when we are healthy, more of us would exercise moral imagination and take on the viewpoint of the suffering.

Most animal rightists live in a blessed time when, short of contracting serious injury or illness, they can live out their convictions with little apparent risk to their health and well-being. Liberated from the fear of many viruses, freed from the pains of injuries and infections, and spared many of the ravages of disease by the miracles of modern surgery, they have plenty of good health to allow them to complain about the "evils" of research.

The question is, should they complain, or should they, in the name of ethical consistency, refuse vaccinations, painkillers, surgical procedures, and medical advice that come from animal research? Vegetarianism exacts no price; being opposed

---

ANIMAL RIGHTS ID

I,_____,
                    (signature)

hereby identify myself as a supporter of animal rights, and I agree to live my life in accordance with all animal rights principles, especially the principle on the reverse side of this card.

I hereby request that in the event of an accident or illness, all medical treatments developed or tested on animals be withheld, including, but not limited to:

blood transfusions	anesthesia
pain killers	antibiotics
insulin	vaccines
chemotherapy	reconstructive surgery
coronary bypass surgery	CPR
orthopedic surgery	etc.

Figure 6.1 ID card for an animal rightist

to biomedical research involves one in willful ignorance of the source of one's own health or in deliberate ethical inconsistency.

Some propose that animal rights advocates carry a medical emergency card (see Figure 6.1) stipulating that listed treatments dependent on animal research not be undertaken on their behalf.

There are some, of course, who, in the name of ethical consistency, do intend to reject all medical benefits coming from research with animals. Animal rights philosopher Gary Francione is one of them. He draws a peculiar line on this issue. He allows us to use vaccines and medicines that continue to come from triumphs of biomedical science, but closes the door on our children and their children to similar treatments that can be expected for emerging viruses and still untreatable diseases (Francione 1995, 180–81). The past is water under the bridge. And the future? Evidently, we don't need to consider those who live downstream. So it seems that not even Francione, who relishes his moral superiority, has chosen the high road. The fact is, the high road doesn't exist.

Talk show hosts frequently ask why animal rightists and animal researchers can't find some middle ground. The question seems reasonable enough, especially since most people take pride in the politics of compromise. The only hitch is that researchers staked out the middle ground of common sense long ago. On that middle ground we find three of every four Americans, who approve of the use of animals in the search for medical knowledge and cures, demanding only that the scientific community guarantee humane treatment of those animals. On that middle ground we also find animal advocates who believe that we should be working not for animal rights but for animal welfare—to ensure that animals don't suffer and that their necessary deaths are swift and painless.

Colin Blakemore, whom we have already met as an Oxford University scientist targeted by animal terrorists, has considered resigning from his position as head of England's Medical Research Council because cabinet-level officials in the government have sidetracked his nomination to knighthood. Politicians withdrew his name from candidacy for knighthood only because they feared his nomination might alienate Labour

Party support from the animal rights lobby. The truth that the government wanted to keep as a "dirty little secret" is that Blakemore uses animals in his scientific investigations (Leppard).

Blakemore doesn't want that to be a "dirty little secret." Despite having had his name on an extremist hit list, having intercepted letter bombs intended for his children, and having had windows broken at his home, he speaks out publicly and persuasively in favor of humane animal research. He knows that if he hides his work and honors government cowardice with silence, medical research and human (as well as animal) health will be further compromised (McKie [1]).

Another famous researcher, American heart surgeon Michael DeBakey, has said, "It is the American public who will decide whether we must tell hundreds of thousands of victims of heart attacks, cancer, AIDS, and other dread diseases that the rights of animals supersede a patient's right to relief from suffering and premature death" (DeBakey). What the American public decides depends on telling the "dirty little secret" about the animal extremist and animal rights movement, and the "dirty little secret" about the accomplishments and promises of animal research.

BENEFICIARIES OF ANIMAL RESEARCH

"No cures in forty years," has been a battle cry in demonstrations outside our center. You know what? The protesters are exactly right! (Do we hear cheers as animal rightists consider the prospect of quoting THAT out of context?)

Developing "cures" is not the job of *basic* researchers. Their task is the creation of new knowledge. Pharmaceutical companies take that knowledge and use it to design drugs. Understanding how the body works is very different from the process of designing a drug. The latter involves chemists working to control the rate at which drugs are degraded, and biologists and physicians testing potential products for safety and efficacy on animals.

Animal rightists go to great lengths to provide "evidence" that humane animal research is not valuable. With startling audacity they reinvent the great stories of biomedical triumphs—penicillin, polio, diabetes—as if they believe that people will fall victim to a big untruth as long as it is told again and again.

Penicillin

One of the most curious contentions of the animal rights movement is that animal research wasn't initially or integrally part of the history of penicillin (USA Doctors). Nothing could be more straightforward than the statement of Howard Florey, one of the three scientists awarded the Nobel Prize for developing penicillin. "The revolution brought about by antibiotics," he noted, "could not have taken place but for carefully planned and executed animal experiments" (Florey, 4). What's going on here?

Most often, animal rightists seize on two points to question the role that animal research played in the penicillin story. First, there is the element of chance. In 1928, Alexander Fleming was studying staphylococcus in his laboratory at St. Mary's Hospital in London. Returning from a holiday, he noticed that a mold of a bacterium called penicillium was growing on one of his plates where it had evidently destroyed a culture of the staphylococcus. The ability of what Fleming named penicillin to kill disease-causing bacteria had been discovered quite by chance.

That Fleming had not proceeded by design with animals, but had made his discovery by accident in a culture dish, probably explains why animal rights veterinarian Nedim Buyukmihci maintained in debate that animal research was not integral or pivotal to the development of penicillin.[1] The lesson to be learned from the penicillin story, however, is about the interplay of chance and design in scientific advance, and this lesson reinforces rather than diminishes the need for animal research (Speth).

Any school child who has heard about Isaac Newton and the apple knows that the history of science is filled with serendipitous events that start a line of inquiry and discovery.

And that same child, realizing that falling apples had probably hit many others who had never wondered about gravity before Newton, understands the force of Louis Pasteur's comment: chance favors the prepared mind.

Fleming's mind, unfortunately, was not as prepared as Newton's. He pursued his chance discovery only so far as to determine that the antibacterial broth he had on his plates was not harmful to rabbits and mice. Following a hunch rather than submitting that hunch to animal experiments, he decided that penicillin would work best as an antiseptic for skin surface infections. His omission of further animal tests delayed the development of penicillin drugs until a decade later, when Florey and Ernest Chain began systematic experiments in which they injected three of eight streptococcus-infected mice with penicillin. Only the three injected mice survived. Not only was penicillin not toxic to the mice, but also it had cleared their infection.

Florey and Chain went on to produce enough penicillin to begin trials in several patients desperately ill with similar infections. In 1942, an American named Anne Miller benefited from the first penicillin "miracle," recovering completely from blood poisoning that had brought her within hours of death. Soon afterwards, the U.S. Army began five hundred separate clinical trials in military hospitals. Once the war ended, penicillin went into mass production, the first of the "wonder drugs" that have become so much a part of the lives and health of baby boomers and their children.

The second reason that animal rightists try to make penicillin their story grows out of the fact that Florey and Chain were lucky in their choice of research subject. Writing about his research, Florey said:

> Mice were used in the initial toxicity tests because of their small size, which economized the precious material (penicillin), but what a lucky chance it was, for in this respect man is like the mouse and not the guinea pig. If we had used guinea pigs exclusively, we should have said that penicillin was toxic, and we probably should not have proceeded to try and overcome the

difficulties of producing the substance for trial in man, difficulties that seem to me now in retrospect even more fantastic
than they did at the time. (Florey, 12)

Animal rightists take these words as proof that animal
experimentation could have caused penicillin to be discarded
and therefore, by implication, that we should not rely on animal research. In other words, because in this case it *could* have
failed, we should not conduct animal research. Thomas Edi-
son, the Wright brothers, NASA, Jonas Salk—all could have
failed, but the fact is that they didn't. Step from the purely
speculative world of what *could* happen into the real world of
what *does* happen, and we find the mouse protection test
proving penicillin to be an effective antibiotic ready for clinical trials in humans.

The fact that various species differ from each other is both
a risk and an opportunity for researchers. In some fortuitous
respects, the mouse resembles humans; in others, as discovered later, the guinea pig is a more helpful model. Three years
after Florey's mice experiments, a scientist named Dorothy
Hamre discovered that "when treated with the same dose of
penicillin . . . as that given to humans, guinea pigs did not die,
and, in fact, failed to show any signs of toxicity" (Botting, 6).
Her discovery led to studies in 1955 that allowed scientists to
fully explain the cause of the initial toxicity—guinea pigs were
responding to penicillin in a way similar to those human patients
who develop colitis after oral or systemic administration of
antibiotics. Guinea pigs, it turned out, have their own value as
research models in the field of antibiotics. The lesson of Lady
Luck is that researchers have to determine how one species or
another is the appropriate model for their investigations.

If Florey had used guinea pigs, and if his experiments had
yielded evidence of the toxicity of penicillin, advances in the
development of antibiotics might have been delayed but not
halted forever. Some fifty year earlier, Louis Pasteur had predicted that someday bacteria could be used to fight bacteria.
The only thing that could have put an end to that dream
would have been the ban on animal research.

There is an interesting footnote to the penicillin story. Contemporaries of Pasteur such as Sir John Burdon-Sanderson and Thomas Huxley observed and commented on the ability of certain penicillium molds to prevent the growth of bacteria in culture some fifty years before Florey. Why didn't they develop penicillin? It was a question of timing. In the 1870s, the germ theory of disease transmission was still being debated. Only after Robert Koch demonstrated that anthrax bacteria taken from infected animals and injected into healthy animals caused the healthy ones to develop anthrax, could scientists think of applying the properties of penicillium mold to destroy infectious agents. But Koch's experiments would never have been allowed if animal rightists of that time had had their way. Thanks to decades of basic research with animals, not just the minds of Fleming, Florey and Chain, but the whole world of medical research was prepared to seize on the opportunity presented by chance when, in 1928, spores in the air accidentally infected Fleming's plate of staphylococcal bacteria.

Thalidomide

The fact that many animal advocates deny the importance of animal research in the development of penicillin is indeed curious. But when some of them, including Peter Singer, blame animal research for the tragedy of thalidomide, a drug that caused ten thousand children to be born crippled or deformed in the 1960s, things get "curiouser" (Singer [1], 50–51). Even though John McArdle, PhD, once a scientific advisor to the animal rights movement, warned that the true story about thalidomide favors using animals in toxicity testing, partisans of the animals rights movement continue to repeat Singer's opinion that "what we should learn from thalidomide . . . is not that animal testing is necessary, but that it is unreliable" (McArdle, 57).

The facts are not disputed. After tests on rats and other laboratory animals revealed no ill effects, thalidomide was introduced in many countries as a sedative in 1957. In the United States, however, an FDA official named Frances Kelsey fought successfully to keep it off the market. She was convinced that testing had not been sufficiently extensive. In 1960, the drug began to be prescribed in Europe to control morning sickness during pregnancy, and a year later it became apparent from the births of impaired babies that something was dreadfully wrong. By the end of 1961, thalidomide had been removed from the market, and in the very next year Congress passed the Food, Drug and Cosmetics Act of 1962 to increase the powers of the FDA to guarantee drug safety.

All agree that thalidomide wasn't tested on pregnant animals until after women taking the drug began giving birth to deformed babies. Then it was found to cause birth defects in rabbits and several types of monkeys. Disagreement turns on whether more extensive testing would have detected this problem. Animal rightists seem to take their cue from a report of the Office of Health Economics, a research organization set up by the Association of the British Pharmaceutical Industry: "With thalidomide . . . it is only possible to produce the specific deformities in a very small number of species of animals. In this particular case, therefore, it is unlikely that specific tests in pregnant animals would have given the necessary warning: the right species would probably never have been used" (Teeling-Smith, 29).

Notice the words "specific deformities." Neal Barnard and Stephen Kaufman employ similar qualifying language when they say, "Most animal species used in laboratories do not develop *the kind of limb defects* [emphasis added] seen in humans after thalidomide exposure; only rabbits and some primates do" (Barnard and Kaufman, 82). However, as Adrian Morrison points out, Barnard and Kaufman ignore the fact that subsequent tests in the early 1960s with mice, rats, and certain inbred strains of hamsters showed congenital malformations of eyes, ears, heart, kidneys, and digestive tracts (Botting and Morrison [2]). Surely, if such results had been available before, rather than after, approval of thalidomide in Europe, its introduction would have been delayed for the further trials demanded by Kelsey, trials conducted in many species of pregnant animals that would have given the necessary warning about the specific deformities that occurred in humans.

The real question, according to Morrison, is whether "thalidomide [would] pass the [birth defect] tests subsequently implemented as a result of the tragedy, if it were produced as a new chemical entity today?" He answers his own question with an emphatic no. And, on this point, McArdle agrees: "If tested under today's standards, thalidomide's potential to cause birth defects would probably be discovered" (McArdle, 57).

Polio

The attack on animal research becomes "curiouser and curiouser" when it comes to the story of the polio vaccine. In the millennia before vaccination, it seemed that diseases ebbed and flowed like sea tides—breaking out, spending themselves, and then receding for their next assault. The reality was that a disease-causing virus would confer immunity on survivors of its attack, only to later ravage children and grandchildren whose immune systems had not been trained by exposure to recognize the enemy.

One such microbe was the poliovirus. The disease it causes—poliomyelitis, or infantile paralysis—has been traced back as far as early Egyptian civilization. Polio injures the myelin sheath of nerve cells, which coats nerves somewhat as insulation protects electrical wiring. Myelin damage brings about symptoms as mild as neck and back stiffness and as severe as paralysis. Since the virus is spread by swallowing water contaminated with human body wastes, the number of polio cases began to decline with the steady improvement in sanitation during the last half of the nineteenth century. Despite this general and gradual decline, however, serious polio epidemics broke out in many different places in the first fifty years of the twentieth century. The most devastating, occurring in 1952, affected fifty-eight thousand Americans, half of whom were paralyzed. Ironically, better sanitation had slowed the spread of the virus but had left many older children and adults, who were no longer exposed to mild forms of the disease during infancy, vulnerable to debilitating and life-threatening infection.

Medical science, which, like art, imitates nature, had already learned how to mimic and improve on nature's method of building up immunity to smallpox. In the early 1900s, it set out to do the same for polio. Its task was to replace and improve on the immunity that was being lost as an unintended side effect of covering sewers and purifying drinking water. Scientists hoped to design a vaccine that would not just curtail the poliovirus—as nature had—but eliminate the threat of polio forever.

Before that could happen, much would have to be learned. First, it would be necessary to prove that polio is, indeed, an infectious disease. This was accomplished in 1909 when scientists brought about polio lesions by grinding up spinal cord tissue of paralyzed children who died and transferring it to monkeys, which then became sick. Next, it would be necessary to determine the route of infection and progression of the disease. Swedish scientists, using a monkey assay in a study of fourteen cases of polio during the outbreak of 1911, learned that the poliovirus gains access to the nervous system through the gastrointestinal tract.

Third, it would be necessary to grow large quantities of the virus for the production of a pure and dosage-exact vaccine. Facilitated by the development of antibiotics in the early 1940s, John Enders, Frederick Robbins, and Thomas Weller succeeded in growing the poliovirus in human, non–nerve cell cultures in 1949. Their achievement, for which they received the Nobel Prize for Medicine in 1954, was based on information from previous animal research, used animal serum in cell cultures, and demonstrated its success by injection of the virus into mice and monkeys.

Fourth, it would be important to identify all possible variants of the virus against which the vaccine would have to be effective. This task, which was completed in 1949 with the classification of three distinct strains of poliovirus, was conducted with monkeys. Fifth, improvements would have to be made in diagnosing infection, killing and deactivating viruses, and designing trial protocols.

Finally, by 1954, the stage was set, and massive immunization trials proved the efficacy of a killed-virus vaccine prepared by Jonas Salk. Two years later, Albert Sabin's live, attenuated-virus oral vaccine was also shown to be successful in preventing polio infection, first in monkeys, then in humans. Both vaccines are still derived from monkey kidney tissue and tested for safety and efficacy in monkeys. Today, at least in industrialized nations, the signs warning against swimming in public pools and the pictures of hospital wards filled with iron lungs, which allowed affected and paralyzed children to breathe, are all but forgotten.

It is clear that monkeys were involved at every stage in polio research. Nevertheless, Neal Barnard and Stephen Kaufman, writing in the prestigious *Scientific American*, have contended that animal experimentation delayed the fight against polio (Barnard and Kaufman, 80). They rely on 1984 congressional testimony by Albert Sabin, who acknowledged that American scientists working with monkeys misled researchers about the route of poliovirus infection for three decades. Sabin subsequently explained his remark: even though his testimony was correctly quoted, it was wrongly interpreted. Primate studies, he said, "were necessary to solve many problems before an oral polio virus vaccine could become a reality" (Sabin). It was true that American researchers worked for thirty years on a theory of infection that eventually was disproved, but it was the theory and not the use of monkey models that led them astray.

Commenting on the claims of Barnard and Kaufman, Frederick Robbins, one of the three Nobel laureates honored for work on polio, said, "The statement that animal experimentation delayed the 'fight against polio' is totally wrong. . . . Far from misleading us, animals led us to the truth and made possible the eventual solution" (Foundation for Biomedical Research [1]).

You might think that the claim about polio would be dropped, but animal rightists continue to quote Dr. Kaufman to this day. They range from Theodora Capaldo, president of the Ethical Science and Education Coalition (Capaldo), to Elaine Close, the friend of Craig Rosebraugh (Close).

AIDS

Ray Greek, MD, whom we met in Chapter 2, cites Mark Feinberg, a leading AIDS researcher:

> What good does it do you to test something [a vaccine] in a monkey? You find five or six years from now that it works in the monkey, and then you test it in humans and you realize that humans behave totally differently from monkeys, so you've wasted five years.
> Monkeys do not die of AIDS. Humans do. (Greek, 203)

When Dr. Feinberg had a chance to speak for himself, he said,

> There are many instances where the use of animal model research is absolutely essential for evaluating the safety and efficacy of [AIDS] candidate vaccines. Moreover, the statement that "Monkeys do not get AIDS; humans do," is completely false. The SIV [simian immunodeficiency virus] infection model for AIDS has been extremely important for understanding critical aspects of AIDS pathogenesis that cannot be studied in humans. I do not wish to be held responsible for comments . . . that have been so removed from their context that they no longer convey the meaning I had intended. (Personal email from Mark Feinberg, MD, PhD, to Charles Nicoll, PhD)

Diabetes

The defects of the pancreas that cause diabetes were first discovered by research in dogs. Leonard Thompson was a fourteen-year-old boy who weighed only sixty-five pounds when admitted with diabetes to the Toronto General Hospital. On

January 23, 1922, he received his second series of injections containing dog pancreatic extract. The signs of diabetes all but vanished, he "became brighter, more active, looked better, and said he felt stronger." Historian Michael Bliss continues:

> Those who watched the first starved, sometimes comatose, diabetics receive insulin and return to life saw one of the genuine miracles of modern medicine. They were present at the closest approach to the resurrection of the body that our secular society can achieve, and at the discovery of what has become the elixir of life of millions of human beings around the world. (Bliss, 11)

Consider, however, Brandon Reines, who has written a pamphlet for the American Anti-Vivisection Society entitled *The Truth Behind the Discovery of Insulin*. Mr. Reines cited Bliss's 1982 book, *The Discovery of Insulin*, as the source for his view that the animal experimentation that preceded the discovery of insulin was not part of the scientific process that led to insulin. When Mr. Bliss got a chance to speak for himself, he didn't mince words: "Reines' interpretation of my work is thoroughly distorted, wrong-headed and silly. . . . The discovery of insulin in the early 1920s stands as one of the outstanding examples in medical history of the successful use of animal experimentation to improve the human condition" (Foundation for Biomedical Research [2]).

An important footnote to the story of diabetes is that animal research advances human medicine, which, in turn, helps pets and farm animals. The older of my two dogs now receives daily injections of life-saving *human* insulin.

So it goes. These are not the only examples of a strategy called "out-of context quoting." With computer scissors and glue, activists can take any statement out of context and make it look like another bit of evidence that animal research is useless. By the time the original authors or an occasional alert reader has caught up with them, the damage has been done. The public is confused by charge and countercharge, and the big "untruth" appears plausible.

Perhaps, however, truth would prevail in debates that animal rights activists sometimes call loudly for. We were perplexed for a time that people knowledgeable about the importance of animal research avoided such interactions. Their reluctance is based on the definition of debate.

When we think of debating, we think spontaneously of the generally civil interactions at political debates hosted by the League of Women Voters. One side speaks, and then the other. Debates with animal rightists are different: they are shouting matches, complete with verbal accusations and name-calling. Animal rightists seldom know about research oversight by Institutional Animal Care and Use Committees (IACUCs), and they don't want to hear about them. They have come with preconceptions and prejudices that they don't wish to subject to scrutiny. What they are seeking is a kind of street theater, media coverage, and public attention.

During my experience on the East Coast, I attempted to interact with animal rightists whom the search committee—and Florida law—had allowed into the room to ask "a few questions." The first question was, "Why does your laboratory torture animals?" I thought that I had a rock-solid response, "I do not use animals in my lab." Their knee-jerk response was, "Why are you lying?" The presumptions were that I used animals, tortured them, and was lying. There was no meaningful debate or exchange of ideas, but that snippet was the part that the cameramen loved and the producers put on the TV news that night.

Former Surgeon General C. Everett Koop won the esteem of the public for his forthright pronouncements on various health risks. Koop's most valuable contribution might have been this caution: *The animal rights movement is dangerous to our health.* This warning, if placed on prescription pads, organ donor cards, and hospital admission forms, could help shield us from the "big untruth." It refocuses our attention on the researchers and doctors who try to set the record straight on how we got the polio vaccine, insulin, and organ transplants or on how our children could be better protected from cystic fibrosis, muscular dystrophy, cancer, heart disease, AIDS, and Alzheimer's. The "how," of course, is through the humane use of animals in basic biomedical research.

CHAPTER 7

YES, BUT WHAT ABOUT . . .

Besides looking at how animal rightists and extremists operate, we've outlined five interlocking strategies of the larger animal rights community: (1) intimidating university researchers, administrators, donors, and vendors; (2) misrepresenting research; (3) recruiting children; (4) identifying itself with environmentalism; and (5) calling for the recognition of animals as legal persons. It is this last strategy that we want to examine in more depth. It is time to talk specifically of the rights of animals.

THE RIGHTS OF ANIMALS?
THE GAP BETWEEN US

Like so many of the characters profiled in this book, Doug Cress, who heads the Great Ape Project (GAP), works in Portland, Oregon. His project is to bring absolute equality to all great apes—that's chimpanzees, gorillas, orangutans, and you and me.

The dogma inspiring this project was defined in a 1995 book, *The Great Ape Project: Equality Beyond Humanity*, a collection of essays edited by Paola Cavalieri, a freelance writer, and Peter Singer. Contributors include field biologists, psychologists, lawyers, philosophers, and anthropologists.

Renowned observer of the Gombe Stream National Park chimpanzees, Jane Goodall, leads off with a plea to recognize human and chimpanzee similarities in legal protections. Roger and Deborah Fouts, co-directors of the Chimpanzee and Human Communication Institute, follow with a report on the communication skills of chimps, especially Washoe, who they believe learned sign language. Bernard Rollins, who developed the first college course in veterinary ethics and animal rights, suggests that the first step to primate equality is to prohibit the importing of apes for zoos, entertainment, or research.

The book contains a "Declaration on Great Apes," a remarkably terse statement, given the far-ranging ramifications of the proposal:

We demand the extension of the community of equals to include all great apes: human beings, chimpanzees, bonobos, gorillas, and orangutans.

The community of equals is the moral community within which we accept certain basic moral principles or rights as governing our relations with each other and enforceable at law. Among these principles or rights are the following:

1. The Right to Life
The lives of members of the community of equals are to be protected. Members of the community of equals may not be killed except in very strictly defined circumstances, for example, self-defence.

2. The Protection of Individual Liberty
Members of the community of equals are not to be arbitrarily deprived of their liberty; if they should be imprisoned without due legal process, they have the right to immediate release. The detention of those who have not been convicted of any crime, or of those who are not criminally liable, should be allowed only where it can be shown to be for their own good, or necessary to protect the public from a member of the community who would clearly be a danger to others if at liberty. In such cases, members of the community of equals must have the right to appeal, either directly or, if they lack the relevant capacity, through an advocate, to a judicial tribunal.

3. The Prohibition of Torture
   The deliberate infliction of severe pain on a member
   of the community of equals, either wantonly or for an
   alleged benefit to others, is regarded as torture, and is
   wrong. (Cavalieri, 4)

Among great ape principles and rights are those of life, liberty, and protection of liberty. Are there other rights? That isn't clear, and judging from one discussion of the right to vote (Sapontzis, 273–74), we don't expect that apes have that right or, for example, the right to drive vehicles. The organization Psychologists for the Ethical Treatment of Animals clarifies the central dogma as follows:

Apes would no longer be objects, things, or chattel, but considered as persons. The argument is that apes have both the ability to relate with others and to demonstrate consciousness. . . .

It was not long ago that groups within our own species were considered not having enough human qualities to deserve many rights. In certain societies this included: slaves, women and children, the retarded or developmentally impaired, the insane or emotionally impaired, people of other colors, gays and lesbians, and the physically challenged were once considered not quite human and therefore deserving of little or no rights.

Some animal welfare activists are concerned that only apes were chosen for membership in the human community. The authors of this project agree, but believe this is a start that has solid evidence which supports these apes being so close to humans that they may be considered as such. (Psychologists for Ethical Treatment of Animals)

Singer has made famous a word coined by one of his animal rights colleagues—speciesism. Like racism or sexism, speciesism is a bias that views and treats members of one group differently than members of another group for no reason except membership in the group—in this case, membership in the human species. Lest we be guilty of speciesism, we should include great apes with humans in a community of equals because there is no justification other than our membership in the human species for excluding them. Indeed, all primates share very much the same genes and manifest very similar behaviors. Let's consider each of these assertions.

First, the claim that human and great ape DNA is so similar appears widely in the animal rights literature. It is cited as the biological and most easily verifiable basis for the intuition of some people that humans and chimps are virtually the same. Accurate insofar as it is stated, its meaning and implications are questionable.

It is not surprising that there is overlap in human and chimpanzee DNA. After all, the fundamental processes of life—enzymes that metabolize sugar, build amino acids, and assemble protein—are identical. Fundamental proteins such as the histones that regulate genetic expression or the P450 enzymes that detoxify what we ingest are very similar in virtually all animals and, for that matter, in plants, too. All life on earth is similar, having ties in an evolutionary history—or, if you reject evolution, a wise deity who learns from mistakes. No species discards the lessons of prior species; rather, all build on the preceding experience.

We can't write off the importance of that 1.5 percent of human DNA that doesn't overlap. The human genome is 3 billion base pairs long. That means there are 45 million (1.5 percent x 3 billion) genetic differences between humans and chimps—hardly trivial. That "blueprint information," if printed out would run to a hundred fairly lengthy books, or, if you prefer, technical manuals. It will be the work of the next decade of science to identify the differences and understand what it is that gives humans, but not chimps, the ability to take responsibility for their actions.

It is also important to understand that major sections of the genome can be turned off and on by other relatively small sequences of DNA. For this reason, commonality of DNA does not mean identity in the activity of genes—not even close. Consider the following two sentences:

1. Animals are just like humans and do deserve identical rights, responsibilities, and privileges.

2. Animals aren't just like humans and don't deserve identical rights, responsibilities, and privileges.

The homology or agreement in written information is about 95 percent, but the meaning is strikingly different. In bingo, a card with 99 percent homology with the winning card is worthless. Moreover, because there are large areas of genomes, human and ape, that are never expressed, even absolute homology—the 98.5 percent figure that includes such nonexpressed areas—has little significance.

Also we must remember that while our DNA is identical in hair, bone, and muscle cells, its "differential expression" results in very different looking (and acting) cells. A single mutation can change a healthy cell to a cancerous one—a complete alteration in its direction with a change of only one out of our three billion base pairs (which leaves a homology of over 99.99999 percent). It is well known that even a single amino acid change in a protein (less than 1 percent) can alter the action or cellular location of that protein. DNA homology, or even identity, is not a good predictor of similarity on the level of the whole individual.

By the way, did we mention that we humans are also highly homologous with fruit flies and 67 percent genetically identical to worms? We may be monkeys' uncles, but we are also flies' cousins and worms' nephews!

Second, do great apes really share with us behavioral abilities that are relevant to considering them as persons having rights? Relevant abilities would make it possible for our next of kin to take responsibility for their behavior, the responsibility that goes along with rights.

No one would deny that great apes—most all species, for that matter—are conscious. Still, we can ask if they are aware of themselves having to make decisions for which they will be held accountable.

No one would deny that great apes and other species have emotions, but we can ask if they are aware of themselves feeling innocent and guilty.

No one would deny that great apes and other species interact, but we can ask if they are aware of themselves relating responsibly to each other.

No one would deny that great apes and other species are intelligent. Even marsh tits and chickadees store and retrieve food from hundreds of caches; rats rely on a skill something like counting to consistently look for food behind a third door, where they had found food previously; dogs bark when they want to go out; and virtually all mammals show elaborate mating behaviors that likely evolved to preclude wasted efforts of interspecies breeding. We can ask, however, if animals, including great apes, are aware of themselves wondering, puzzling, trying to get the point, grasping meaning ("aha"), checking to be sure their understanding is correct, and then making decisions for which they accept responsibility.

Some proponents of the GAP suggest, "Like humans, great apes can solve problems, deceive others, plan ahead, and make moral judgments." OK, but crows deceive, bees store honey for the winter, and we've seen chickens play poker at the state fair. About the moral judgment . . . wait, tell us again why we aren't letting them vote?

The widely touted "use of tools" in the nonhuman primate world is pretty much limited to using sticks, a behavior that requires these animals to apply a perceived spatial pattern— this stick is longer than my finger—to an instinctive behavior of probing anthills. As James Trefil comments, "Anyone who calls the difference between the ability to build a Boeing 747 (or even the ability to build a fire) and the ability to use a stick just a matter of degree is willfully obtuse" (Trefil, 38). There is invention and there is invention.

Finally, no one would deny that great apes and other animals communicate, but we can ask if a learned behavior of getting a banana—whether it is by pressing a lever or by making a sign—is the same thing as speaking a language. It may, at most, be a matter of using rather than understanding and speaking a language. To use a language is to employ signs or pictures or even words to fulfill a demand, obtain a reward, or achieve a desired end; to understand language is to employ the same instruments not just as means to ends, but also as a way to reveal activities in one's mind and in the minds of others. Computers can be programmed to use words. What they can't do is grasp the meaning of words in others' minds.

Language experts, including Steven Pinker, are convinced that our next of kin fall far short of the communication skills of human children, who, at about the age of three and without specific training, explode with language (Pinker, 271–277). The explosion is more than a rapid increase of vocabulary. Children go beyond the mere use of words to an understanding of thousands of words and the rules for joining them in an infinite number of novel combinations that express ideas. The reason for their astonishing ability is that they grasp the meaning of words in others' minds. For them, a word is not just a sign, or one thing standing for another, but a symbol, or a framework into which human minds can read significance. Sociologist Alan Wolfe expands on sign and symbol when he observes: "Brains, including artificially created ones as well as complex ones found among primates, can manipulate signs; but, because the meaning of a symbol does not exist within the symbol but has to be interpreted by a mind, only a species capable of interpretation can attribute meaning to a symbol" (Wolfe, 79).

In addition to the arguments from genes and behavior, animal rightists frequently ask how we can guarantee the rights of infants and the mentally impaired but deny them to nonhuman primates that have the same or even greater capacities. But young children do grow into adults and chimps grow into . . . chimps. In the case of mentally impaired individuals something has gone sadly wrong with typical development. The grief and the pity we experience in the presence of such fellow humans reveal that we view them quite differently than animals lacking the same capacities. It is normal for a gorilla to have the abilities of a gorilla.

Not long before editing *The Great Ape Project*, Singer spelled out the logical implications of the book in his own *Rethinking Life and Death*. "Those [nonhuman] beings who qualify as 'persons,'" he noted, "most conclusively are great apes, although "whales, dolphins, elephants, monkeys, dogs, pigs and other animals may eventually . . . have to be considered as persons" (Singer [4], 182). Even if none of the contributors to *The Great Ape Project* urged the status of personhood and rights for all animals, the logic of their position leads in that direction. Consider animal behaviorist Marian Dawkins:

> Pigeons and parrots are now being acclaimed for their hitherto undreamed of cognitive capacities. Meanwhile, research on various other kinds of birds, including chickens, has revealed similar findings that demand a revision of demeaning stereotypes.
>
> With increased knowledge of the behavior and cognitive abilities of the chicken has come the realization that the chicken is not an inferior species to be treated merely as a food source. (Dawkins, 213)

Pigeons, parrots, and chickens seem to be one step from personhood and rights. Even if researchers discover differences between their cognitive abilities and ours, can we exclude them from the "community of equals"? As animal rights philosopher Steven Sapontzis points out, any effort to secure equal footing for great apes, but only great apes, falls into the same speciesist error that animal rightists abhor (Sapontzis, 271). If great ape proponents draw a line between great apes and other animals, then they are drawing such a line on the basis of their greater mental capacities, prizing nonhuman primates simply because they resemble humans. The logic of the GAP proponents can't be halted anywhere in its progress without speciesism raising its ugly head.

Maybe worms and fruit flies will soon have rights. Surely, we are joking. But the jest is not just silly. It highlights one problem with the GAP: where do we stop when recognizing rights for species other than our own? It also brings to mind a host of other problems. If we are to guarantee the rights of the great apes, presumably that includes protecting them from each other. How are we to do that? Can we put them on trial?

Do we police them—not locking them up in cages, of course—by patrolling the rainforest? Of course not. The suspicion grows that the GAP would not so much improve the lot of nonhuman primates and other animals as much as it would threaten and degrade the lives of humans. To grant special protection for endangered chimpanzee or gorilla populations might be well and good; to protect all chimpanzees and gorillas by extending rights to them and, eventually, to all animals, is either nonsense or a carefully devised ploy to bring about an end to any use of animals, including the biomedical research on which both human and animal health depend.

THE RIGHTS OF ANIMALS

Words can mislead—sometimes because the speaker wants them to. It is no surprise that animal rightists label researchers "vivisectors" to sway public opinion. Nor is it a surprise that animal rightists have convinced several cities to change the words "pet *owner*" to "animal *guardian*" in ordinances and statutes. It seems like something meaningless that might make a few people happy without doing any harm. This new usage, however, prejudices *how* we think.

In the strict sense, what can "animal rights" possibly mean? We have seen that Singer scorns the notion of rights. Another philosopher, Tom Regan, not only takes Singer to task, but also labors at length to prove that animals, because they have an awareness of the world around them and desires within them that make them similar to humans, have at least the right not be used by humans for any of our purposes (Regan [1], 330–400). In our opinion, however, Regan's efforts ultimately fail. He acknowledges that animals aren't moral agents (responsible creatures), and his insistence that they are "moral patients," equivalent to marginally human infants, founders on the hard rock of common sense. Spontaneously and easily we grasp the difference between a mentally challenged baby, whom we welcome but grieve, and an animal with the mental life that we look upon as perfectly normal.

We begin to understand the concept of rights when we are children. We realize what we can express years later: one cannot have rights without the ability to take responsibility. At age seven, we weren't allowed to drive because we couldn't take responsibility for our actions. Likewise, animals cannot have rights because they cannot take responsibility for their actions. Animals in the wild are evidence. Monkeys steal, assault, rape, and cannibalize. They don't take responsibility for their actions, and no one expects them to. The raped monkey cannot take the rapist to court. The family of the murdered and cannibalized monkey has no legal recourse. Monkeys live in a world of impunity.

Animal rightists steer clear of the obvious case in which one animal—a cat, for example—kills another—a field mouse. There are no proposals that someone obtain standing on behalf of the late mouse and sue the cat because the mouse's civil rights were violated. It is in the cat's nature to kill the mouse, and the cat cannot take responsibility for its actions. Yet, it is in this "Alice in Wonderland" world that the animal rightists would have us live.

Pursue the case of the cat and mouse. How do you deal with the robin perched nearby which saw the whole assault? Can we put it on the witness stand? Of course, the robin couldn't be sworn in as a witness and address the jury intelligently.

The case is somewhat different for a chimpanzee, however. A chimp might go on the witness stand and, after careful coaching in sign language, employ a series of signs ostensibly attesting to cruel imprisonment in a laboratory. Although a skilled animal behaviorist might see through this act, a judge or a jury might not.

In a world where animals have rights, a laboratory director could be charged with false imprisonment and convicted by a well-meaning jury. Once the legal precedent is established that chimps have rights, why not rhesus monkeys, pigs, rats, and . . . you see the cascade of silliness. A line cannot be drawn. Accept the view that animals have rights even though they can't take responsibility for their actions, and we accept a construct that leads us into . . . utopia? Yes, utopia, a word that means "nowhere," a world of absurdity in which breeding animals is racist, keeping pets is kidnapping, and legitimate animal research is slavery and torture.

THE WELFARE OF ANIMALS

As you are thinking about this, make the distinction between animal rights and our moral responsibility, as humans, to treat animals humanely. We should minimize suffering, and be certain that animals under our care never lack the essentials of life. That is a concept—the concept of animal welfare—that is quite apart from ascribing rights to animals.

The animal rights view is rooted in a way of viewing animals that has become almost a norm in today's society. Because they look a bit like humans, we tend to think of animals as humans. They look so much like us, in fact, that we find it hilarious to see a monkey wearing a diaper or a chimp engaged in outlandish behavior with a talk show host.

At some point, perhaps around the time Disney's Bambi and Thumper were discussing philosophy and expressing their feelings in the woods, we changed our view of all animals. We started thinking about them as furry, four-legged people. Mickey looks much more like a human infant than a mouse, and Snoopy, flying his doghouse as a plane, a scarf trailing behind, appears less like a dog than a human pilot. If we judge by appearances, then we will hold that animal perceptions are like ours. I am being analytical here, but I, too, fall into the trap of projecting human experiences on animals when interacting with my dogs. We want to believe that they think and act like us, just as we want to believe that other humans think like we do.

We frequently conclude that animals look happy or, if they are in the same set of circumstances that make us happy, that they are happy. Not being a monkey, dog, goldfish, or ladybug, we don't know what makes them happy. I assume they prefer to have food and water, and that monkeys like to do what they do in fact do—forage for food, groom each other, and challenge their dominant colleagues even in internecine war. But beyond that I do not know. They do not seem to have an appreciation of Monet's art, a beautiful home, or a charitable deed. Dogs appear as happy smelling dead carcasses as fresh flowers.

Animals are not persons, even if animal rightists would like you to believe they are. Consider America's most beloved pet, the dog. Behavioral studies reveal that it spends most of its time thinking about food. When my dog walks over to me, the best bet is that he anticipates food or a pat on the head. Notice that he always watches my hands while interacting with me; hands are the source of patting and snacks—and that is what he is most interested in. People watch your eyes, seldom your hands—unless you are a magician or holding a gun at them!

Consider, once again, my dog and his daily walk. He jumps up with enthusiasm when it sees me pick up the leash. One day it is raining; does he consider that I look tired and think, "Gee he looks so tired and it is raining, maybe I will pretend that I don't want a walk today, just to be nice"? If you have to think about this for more than a few seconds, you don't know the nature of dogs.

Actually, I have two dogs, very sweet golden retrievers. The younger will periodically roll on fresh deer droppings. I have trouble understanding this behavior; I am not a dog, of course, and so lack the appropriate sensitivity to this need. Dogs, even if well-fed and not vitamin-deprived, are known to eat their own excrement. I don't hear the evolutionary voice that is dictating this behavior.

Often, animal rightists do not understand the needs of animals and conclude, wrongly, that these needs coincide with human needs. Those who lobby for larger cages for rabbits don't know that rabbits appear to prefer small cages, probably because exposure in large spaces frightens them. Those who "liberate" farm-raised mink seem not to know that farm-raised mink lack the skills to survive in the wild. Most are hit by cars, probably because they associate the sound of cars with the carts from which they are fed. Many drown when they seek drinking water in unfamiliar and fast-flowing streams.

Some animal rightists, for example, proudly brag of denying their dogs meat products and putting them on a vegetarian or, worse still, a vegan diet. This denies them their evolutionary heritage and subjects some of them to lives of chronic diarrhea. If dogs have any rights, shouldn't they include the "right" to meat? They have the pointy canine incisors that generations of wolves and coyotes have used to rip the sinews of meat, teeth that millions of years of evolution have shaped for more than chewing carrots. To assume that dogs or monkeys or ladybugs think like humans is wrong. If you believe otherwise, you are doing an injustice to humans, dogs, monkeys, and ladybugs.

It is striking that the people who are the most compassionate toward animals are those who live and work with them. Animal rightists who think that animals are little people—not as bright and a bit furrier, perhaps, but little people, nonetheless—don't understand the nature of animals. Their misunderstanding may be connected to the curious view among some of them that we should use mentally challenged humans instead of monkeys in medical research.

We consider ourselves animal welfarists. We don't ascribe rights to animals, but we do believe that researchers, entertainers, people who raise animals for meat and clothing, and the general public have the responsibility to treat animals humanely and with compassion. We will not tolerate the bad treatment of an animal under our supervision.

If we can get past the "dirty little secret syndrome," we will have to seize every opportunity to clarify for the public that "animal rights" and "animal welfare" are not just two slightly different expressions for the reality of caring about and for animals. They are emphatically not equivalent. Words can mislead. Saying, "Animal rights, animal welfare . . . whatever!" is very misleading—and dangerous.

THE REGULATION OF ANIMAL RESEARCH

About half of the American population polled about animal research is convinced that animal research is unregulated. The fact is that the U.S. Public Health Service Act requires that all scientists receiving research funds from the National Institutes of Health, the Food and Drug Administration, or the Centers for Disease Control adhere to the standards set out in the *Guide for the Care and Use of Laboratory Animals* (National Research Council 1996).

In addition, the Animal Welfare Act (AWA), which was crafted with input from advocates of welfare and biomedical researchers alike, sets standards of animal care for research institutions. Regulations implementing this act set requirements for the housing, feeding, cleanliness, exercise, and medical needs of laboratory animals and stipulate the use of anesthesia or analgesic drugs for potentially painful procedures and during postoperative care. The act is administered by the USDA, whose veterinary agents in the Animal and Plant Health Inspection Service (APHIS) conduct unannounced site visits to research institutions to ensure compliance with regulations.

Both the Public Health Service Act and the Animal Welfare Act require institutions to establish Institutional Animal Care and Use Committees (IACUCs) to ensure that research animals are treated responsibly and humanely. These IACUCs are composed of veterinarians, scientists, lay members (nonscientific personnel), and at least one representative of the public at large. The *Guide* stipulates that public members "not be laboratory-animal users, be affiliated with the institution, or be members of the immediate family of a person who is affiliated with the institution." In our case at the Oregon National Primate Research Center, the public member is a retired high school teacher of biology. His role is delineated in a description summarized from University of Arizona Web site; he is to

- support the animals' interest and to protect animals from painful procedures;

- help deal with the difficult ethical dilemmas that research involving animals poses;
- communicate the public's concerns and conscience; and
- provide straightforward, honest questioning.

IACUCs oversee all research projects with animals. They do not approve specific research proposals until researchers demonstrate that

- they have selected the most appropriate species;
- they will use the minimum number of animals needed to produce scientifically valid results;
- the information sought in the experiments is important enough to the advance of medical knowledge to warrant the use of animals;
- the animals will receive appropriate anesthesia and analgesic drugs for any potentially painful procedures; and
- all procedures and practices are in compliance with the *Guide*, Animal Welfare Act regulations, the NIH Assurance State, and any other regulations or policies that apply.

In addition to reviewing research proposals, IACUCs

- review semiannually the institutional program for animal care and use;
- inspect semiannually the animal facilities and animal-study areas;
- review and approve, or require modifications in or withhold approval of, those components of activities related to the care and use of animals;
- make recommendations to the institutional official regarding any aspect of the animal care program, facilities, or personnel training;
- suspend any animal care and use activity that does not comply with standards and approved protocols; and
- review concerns involving the care and use of animals at the institution.

IACUCs have the authority to halt research in progress if concerns about animal welfare arise. They also have responsibility to determine that scientists, animal technicians, and other personnel involved with animal care treatment and use are qualified by training or experience for their animal-related duties.

The most important of IACUCs responsibilities is to guarantee that procedures avoid or minimize any animal pain. Members must determine that the principal investigator has considered alternatives to procedures that may cause more than the slight or momentary pain caused, for example, by injections. Consideration of alternatives is guided by what is referred to as the 3Rs, replacement, reduction, and refinement. *Replacement* means using

- animals low on the phylogenetic scale, i.e., invertebrates, insects;
- *in vitro* techniques such as organ, tissue, or cell culture;
- nonanimal living systems, i.e., retroviral gene transfer; or
- nonliving systems, i.e., computer modeling.

Reduction means reducing the total number of animals used to the absolute minimum necessary to achieve statistical significance. Reduction may involve preliminary statistical computations and/or computer modeling, animal sharing when tissues or organs are needed, or the elimination of variables that would increase the number of animals needed.

Refinement means modifying an existing procedure or technique so as to minimize the level of pain or distress endured by the animal. Refinement may involve decreasing invasiveness of a procedure or utilizing noninvasive technology, improved technique, or better control of pain or distress.

To obtain IACUC approval for procedures causing more than momentary or slight pain or distress and not alleviated by analgesics or anesthetics, investigators must present written explanations and make compelling cases for the critical nature of their experiments. The written submission includes a description of the methods and sources—the Animal Welfare Information Center is one, for example—that were used to determine that alternatives were not available and that the investigation doesn't unnecessarily repeat previous experiments.

In addition, each year all research institutions must file a report with the USDA on the number of animals in studies that involve no pain or minimal pain, the number used in studies in which pain is involved but appropriate analgesia or anesthesia is used, and the number of animals used in studies in which pain relief is not used because it would have adversely affected the research results. In the last case, the report must include an explanation and justification of the necessity of the painful procedures.

Currently, animal rights activists are seeking to include rats, mice, and birds along with primates, dogs, and cats, which are presently covered under the provisions implementing the Animal Welfare Act. They argue that these species make up over 90 percent of the animals used in research. Scientists respond that in most cases—those cases of NIH-funded research—rats, mice, and birds are covered already by provisions of the Public Health Service Act. They are convinced that inclusion under the AWA would not alter the conditions of these laboratory animals. They also fear that it would bury research institutions under an avalanche of paperwork, an outcome that could well be the aim of the activists.

In addition to the U.S. government, a worldwide, private, nonprofit organization promotes the responsible treatment of animals in science through voluntary accreditation and assessment programs. The Association for the Assessment and Accreditation of Laboratory Animal Care (AAALAC) guarantees that research programs meet the highest standards of care for laboratory animals. There is strong pressure in the veterinary community to submit to AAALAC accreditation and standards.

In summary, what many Americans don't know is that animal research is

- overseen by Institutional Animal Care and Use Committees;
- regulated by the Animal Welfare Act (http://www.aphis.usda .gov/ac/awa.html);
- inspected by the United States Department of Agriculture (http ://www.aphis.usda.gov/ac/);
- guided by assurances and policies of the National Institutes of Health (http://grants2.nih.gov/grants/olaw/olaw.htm);
- most often accredited by the Association for Assessment and Accreditation of Laboratory Animal Care International (http:// www.aaalac.org/); and

- subject to relevant policies and regulations of the U.S. Centers for Disease Control, the U.S. Fish and Wildlife Service, the Convention on International Trade in Endangered Species, and the International Air Transport Association.

It is not surprising that so many people don't know how comprehensive and detailed the regulation of animal research is. There is a good chance that the majority of our readers waded just a little way into the sea of policies and rules outlined in this chapter and then decided to skip to something more exciting. These policies and rules are not going to make the evening news, but you can bet that an allegation of animal research cruelty, no matter how unfounded, will be at the top of the hour.

CHAPTER 8

PEACE AT LAST?

W e have seen that animal researchers risk intimidation by email and phone campaigns, home visits and picketing, chalking and spray painting of the sidewalks in front of their homes, and leafleting of neighbors. They also live in fear for their families. They are learning to expect that their children may be harassed at school and even used as pawns on the Internet.

Six years ago, Emory University investigator Dr. Kim Wallen discovered one day that animal extremists had posted an image of him with his two young sons on their Web site. He wrote them to explain that the image was copyrighted and to offer them an alternative image of himself alone:

Dear Madam/Sir,

I notice that you are using my copyrighted photo from my Emory Web page on your revamped Web site page on my research. I do not mind that you have my picture on your Web site. However, given the history of an antivivisection fringe that see attacking researcher's families as an appropriate response to their concerns about animal use, I ask that you cease and desist posting the picture with my children. I have chosen to do animal research, they have not. You and I disagree about the value of such research, but I hope that you agree that children are not part of this discussion.

I am attaching a more recent photograph of myself that you may use on your Web site. I will take your removal of the photo of my family as evidence that your group is honorable and ethical and that your primary interest is the animals and not harm to humans that you disagree with. (Wallen)

One would expect that Wallen succeeded in his modest request. But Jean Barnes ("the Barnestormer"), who operates the offending Web site, attempted to negotiate the issue and left images of the children online for months (Wallen).

UNITED WE STAND

With this kind of personal abuse, one might think that researchers could rely on their employers to come to their aid. And yet, as we have seen in the case of Podell, scientists rarely receive help from their institutions, whose very reputations are built on their research prowess. Universities seldom budget anything for educating the community about the value of research and avoid telling the public that animal research is a major component of their research activity. They are silent, hoping that the problem will go away. Professional societies, likewise, avoid addressing issues of animal research. They simply do not wish to become lightning rods for a response from the animal rights community.

Pharmaceutical companies, which depend on animal research to develop products and test their safety, usually subcontract this activity, and confidentiality clauses protect their names. They never produce annual reports that have pictures of animals in cages. They even tout that some products were developed without animal testing. (Usually and thankfully, such products are made of components that have been individually tested.) It is as if all medications, treatments, and medical knowledge drop down from the sky, packaged and ready for health-giving application. They have nothing to do with decades of basic research, much of it with animals.

We thought at one time that we could help educate people about the value of animal research by arranging to have something like this printed on the prescription pads used by doctors:

"This medication was developed, in part, due to animal research." We were hoping, of course, that people would connect the dots between animal research and their own lives. We received immediate negative feedback from professional societies, physicians, and pharmacists. All insisted that many people just don't want to know that animal research is the source of their medications and some patients might not take their pills if they knew.

Would it be a bad thing if patients had to know where their medications come from and if animal rights sympathizers among them could face squarely the consequences of their beliefs? It is an odd paradox of the animal rights movement that many of its partisans abstain from wearing raccoon coats and some from eating meat, but most take advantage of vaccinations, drugs, and surgical techniques, all developed in animals.

At least we can say this: the strategy of silence positions animal research as a "dirty little secret" and plays directly into the hands of animal rightists. They build campaigns based on this "shame." I attended a charity dinner a few years ago and was seated at a table with a member of our university's board. He knew me from previous interactions, but only in an administrative context. "I didn't know you also do research," he remarked, trying to be pleasant. I mentioned where I work and the immediate rejoinder was: "Well, let's not talk about *that* at dinner." Another guest immediately began chatting about our local NBA franchise. If our leadership does not understand and appreciate what we do, how can we communicate our work to the public?

Animal rights groups capitalize on hero worship, enlisting celebrities like Paul McCartney, whose first wife and mother both benefited from animal research by accepting therapy for breast cancer; the B-52s; Kim Basinger; Bill Maher; Mary Tyler Moore, who, as a diabetic, benefits from animal research; Woody Harrelson; and Alec Baldwin, who on occasion wears a leather jacket. Recently, Linda Blair of *The Exorcist* fame spoke unsympathetically to *Steppin' Out* magazine about the late Christopher Reeve's tragic horse-riding accident, which left him a quadriplegic: "He started to ride very late in life. Also, he is a tall man, he's top heavy, the horse had no choice—it just had nowhere to go. So it dumped him. Researchers are breaking animals' spines by the thousands in order to find out how to get nerve re-growth" (Blair). It is almost certain that Blair, or someone in her immediate family, will require medical treatment that has its origins and much of its development in animal research, although there will likely be no news release when that happens.

There are few celebrities—Christopher Reeve was an exception—who will counter the heroes on the animal rights team. At one time the former Superman was an animal rights sympathizer, but after his accident and during his long struggle to survive, he and his wife, Dana, made it clear that they respected but didn't agree with Blair's dismissal of rat research into spinal cord injury. Noting that compassion is key to using animals in research, Dana remarked, "It's hard to watch six-year-old children with spinal cord injuries and say, 'No, don't do a medical experiment on a rat.'" She also said "We're great animal lovers, but even greater human being lovers" (Reeve).

The supporters of biomedical research are those who have personally benefited from it. Severely injured and ill persons such as Reeve and Michael J. Fox, a Parkinson's patient, are the strongest supporters. Most of the seriously sick, however, are not well known and don't have the resources to campaign against animal extremists. Often, too, they must conserve what little energy they have for their own struggle for health. It is remarkable that some, like an indefatigable dialysis patient in Seattle named Patty Wood, speak in schools, organize demonstrations, testify in legislatures, and write letters to their newspapers.

One group of patients that is able to come to the defense of animal research is the AIDS community. Early in their infection, AIDS patients still feel well enough to demonstrate. The spokesperson for an activist group named ACT UP, Steve Michael, himself HIV positive, has noted, "Our lives are more important than a bunch of lab rats. People with AIDS need housing, health care, and nutrition. We're trying to stay alive until there's a cure. These people (PeTA members and other animal extremists) have too much time on their hands and too many T-cells (a cell type lacking in AIDS patients that causes immunosuppression)" (Michael).

Another reason for AIDS activism on the research issue is that while cures for diabetes, Parkinson's, multiple sclerosis, muscular dystrophy, and many other diseases remain the dreams and hopes of scientists, many AIDS patients are already staying healthy longer because of medications developed through animal testing. AIDS activists have noted that attacks on AIDS research by animal rights groups severely hamper efforts to develop still more new drugs and vaccines.

In 1989, laboratories at the University of Arizona were raided. The labs were studying *Cryptosporidium*, a bacterium that causes deadly diarrhea in people with damaged immune systems. There is no treatment for this disorder, and *Cryptosporidium* is not a problem limited to AIDS patients. It also ravages people in Third World countries, cancer patients undergoing chemotherapy and others with impaired immune systems. In the Arizona attack, the ALF stole over 1,200 rats, rabbits, and mice. Years of research to develop a treatment and vaccine for *Cryptosporidium* went up in flames (Animal Liberation Front).

ACT UP has joined with researchers, scientists, and other patient advocates suffering from such diseases as breast cancer and diabetes at press conferences and in picketing and civil disobedience actions. In particular, ACT UP targeted the celebrity fund-raisers of animal rights groups. "The Hollywood crowd needs to realize that by supporting groups like P*e*TA, they are killing people with AIDS," noted ACT UP's Michael. "They can't wear a red ribbon and support groups that oppose our efforts for a world without AIDS" (Michael).

The March of Dimes, the American Heart Association, and several voluntary health organizations supporting patients are ardent and, often, financial supporters of animal research. These organizations must walk a fine line between continuing research advocacy, on the one hand, and maintaining their donor base, on the other. Charities that fund animal research are ever under attack from PCRM and other activists. This is a lesson learned and bravely faced by the March of Dimes. Spokesperson Michelle Kling responded to PCRM in the *Fort Worth Star-Telegram*: "Thousands of children are alive today and millions of people are living healthier lives because of advances in treatment and prevention made possible by March of Dimes-funded research involving animals" (Prince).

Telling it like it is, as Ms. Kling did, requires courage. We like to think that we all have that courage, and we pride our-selves on the belief that we live in civilized times. If we see our neighbor being attacked, we believe that we would run to assist him, or, at least, call 9-1-1. But what happens if we receive a flyer proclaiming that our neighbor is an "animal torturer," a flyer complete with pictures of bloody animals and quotes from scientific papers that indicate that our neigh-bor has inserted probes into the brains of monkeys while alive? Are we likely to help our neighbor, whether we know the truth or not, or are we likely to distance ourselves?

Suppose one morning we wake to see two-foot-tall red let-ters on our neighbor's house that say, "MURDERER." What are we likely to do then? As the victims of other hate groups have learned, we will probably keep a safe distance and put our neighbor in a form of social isolation not unlike that of people shunned by some religious groups.

Suppose that we are in a professional organization that has a few members who engage in animal research—totally ethical research, mind you, and federally inspected, approved, and funded—and those members are attacked. Would we feel obliged to help defend them? What if we knew that the cost of defending them was that the anger of the attacking group would then be turned on us?

Suppose that we are administrators of a major university, one whose reputation is built on the value of the research con-ducted by scientists, including ones who use—humanely—animals. The university is bombarded with images that are fabricated, and allegations are made by someone who has come forward as a "whistle blower." Would we be willing to pay the price to fight public opinion, recognizing that state legislators and taxpayers are watching, some just too busy to carefully analyze all the information they are given and others all too ready to believe whatever outlandish lies are presented? Animal rightists and extremists speak with a disproportionately loud voice. They have taken advantage of excellent tools, most of them free. They know how to use the Internet and email. They are masters at manipulating mass communications, or, as Newkirk reportedly put it, they are "press sluts" (Specter). One of the tools they use best is one that we give them: our silence. They are experts at using that silence against us. They really hope that we will be silent. One animal rightist made the mistake of challenging *Seattle Post Intelligencer* columnist Susan Paynter to witness an animal undergoing an experimental procedure before she wrote about the issue. Paynter reported: "Actually, I did just that at the Hope Heart Institute in Seattle not very long ago. And I have remembered the image ever since, including how grateful I felt to that dog and to the researchers there who were working to save human lives" (Paynter).

From the corner into which we box ourselves when we hide "the dirty little secret," we forget the power of Ms. Paynter's message, our message. We also overlook the fact that the majority of the public supports humane animal research. The question is how long this informed and reasonable view will last.

It is time that universities, professional societies, and the pharmaceutical industry accept the responsibility to tell the public about what we do, the safeguards that are in place and the value that comes of the work. People need to know that we wouldn't have antihypertension drugs, antidiabetic drugs, pharmaceuticals for epilepsy, any of the modern antidepressants, or virtually any of the modern surgical techniques without animal research. We lose the opportunity to tell that story of medical advances and hopes, of controls that are in place to minimize animal suffering, and of laboratory animals that receive excellent health care whenever we take the "safe" course and treat research as a "dirty little secret."

HOPE ON THE HORIZON?

When England's famous Oxford University decided in 2003 to invest approximately £18 million ($34 million) to construct a new animal research building, it opened a Pandora's box. Unlike the afflictions that flew from the original box of myth, the woes from this box were demons threatening the perpetuation of disease or, at least, delay in new modes of treatment.

As plans for the new Biomedical Research Facility on South Parks Road were announced, groups like SPEAK (the Oxford protestor successor to SPEAC [Stop Primate Experiments at Cambridge]) began protesting. Well, "protesting" might be an understatement.

In reality, the campaign of intimidation was so intense that it scared the initial contractors off the job. For sixteen months, construction was at a standstill. The university, however, persisted in planning for the facility, and in November 2005, the extremists began their campaign anew. They had good reason to hope for success: protests had led to the cancellation of a very similar laboratory project in Cambridge a year earlier (Pincock).

The construction workers, people we usually think of as being able to take care of themselves, were threatened and insulted by megaphone, photographed, and followed home. They responded by wearing masks. Some said the masks protected them from cold, but others, more candidly, admitted that they were meant to protect their identities.

What the masks didn't protect them from were bombs that went off in cars and fires set by arsonists (Nature Neuroscience [2]; Gosden). Robin Webb warned that even student accommodations were a legitimate target (BBC [4]). Every added precaution—building materials, for example, had to be delivered under the strictest security—created a siege mentality.

Animal rights spokespersons followed the well-used playbook and blamed the damage and violence on a small number of radicals, who, of course, couldn't be identified. Oxford officials, arguing that all employees have the right to work and study in a safe environment, eventually succeeded in getting a court injunction against these threats and acts of vandalism (Pincock).

Seems like a no-brainer, doesn't it?

So simple that even a child could understand it?

In the next section of this chapter, we describe a painting, *Peaceable Kingdom*, and the biblical quote known to have inspired it: "The wolf also shall dwell with the lamb, and the leopard shall lie down with the kid, and the calf and the young lion and fatling together; and a little child shall lead them." In anticipation of that, we would like to introduce the little child; he is wise beyond his years, and he certainly does seem to be doing the leading. His name is Laurie Pycroft, and he lives near Oxford. In February 2006, he was just sixteen, and he was getting in some recreation before his A-level exams. At the time he was thinking a lot about his grandfather, a man whose life, thanks to medical advances, had been happily extended beyond expectations usual for his sickness.

When Pycroft heard of the animal extremist campaign against the new construction at Oxford, he decided he had a calling. He has become the brains behind "Pro-Test," an initiative that produced large public demonstrations and focused public attention on the terrorist events in Oxford. The public sided with his gathering of scientists and local students. The message was clear: regulated animal research is still needed for medical science to advance, and a small number of terrorists will not overturn the law. You can see the result of Pycroft's initiative here: http://www.pro-test.org.uk/

Nice job Laurie!

Pycroft is brave. Certainly braver than the companies that walked away from long-term business relations with HLS at the first sign of danger, braver even than the board of the New York Stock Exchange that was afraid to list this company for fear of threatened reprisals, and braver than all those who pretended there wasn't a problem. Pycroft is also smart; he knows how to get the public on his side. The trick is to stand up straight and tell the truth.

For his trouble, Pycroft began to receive hate mail and threats—thirty within four weeks of starting Pro-Test. "One said, 'We're going to f—ing kill you'" (Asthana). But he wouldn't be intimidated. The police installed a panic button in his family home and advised him "to back down a bit." But, in the face of such advice, he led a march of eight hundred people through Oxford in support of building the lab, and "under banners calling for humans to come first, the crowd chanted: 'No more threats, no more fear, animal research wanted here'" (Asthana).

Simon Festing, executive director of the Research Defence Society and a speaker at Laurie's Pro-Test rally, summed it up quite nicely: "At the moment the mood is very defiant, because most of us have been keeping our heads down for the last 30 years. . . . I think it does mark a new era" (Demopoulos).

Although it is a little too early to tell, Pycroft's spirited brand of offense may be gaining some yardage. The *Economist* opined that

> campaigners for animal rights are losing their long war against scientific experimentation on animals. Public sympathy for the cause is leaching away as the well-publicised antics of a violent few taint the image of the pacific many. New legislation has restricted even peaceful protest; the police have got tougher on bad behaviour; and figures released by the Home Office this week show that animal experiments have reached their highest level in 14 years. Is it the end of an era? (*Economist*)

Universities and charities in the UK have now come out publicly in favor of animal research. The debate in general is becoming less one-sided. One charity that has decided to be open about its own use of animals in research is the British Heart Foundation. John Martin, a leading university researcher, unapologetically states, "I don't believe animals have rights, but we do need to treat them humanely" (*Economist*).

Over twenty thousand joined former Prime Minister Tony Blair in signing a proresearch petition in the UK.

"And a little child shall lead them?" Indeed.

THE PEACEABLE KINGDOM COME HOME

Between 1820 and the time of his death in 1849, Edward Hicks painted over a hundred versions of his now-famous canvas, *The Peaceable Kingdom.* About half his versions have survived to the present day. Trained as a sign maker, Hicks was no stranger to symbolism. Although many of his Quaker associates tried to get Hicks to give up painting for the legitimacy of farming vegetables or raising animals, he persisted, and the series of paintings provides an interesting view of his evolving reflections.

Hicks found inspiration for these paintings in the Bible's description of the end of time (Isaiah, chap. 11). This poetic vision undoubtedly appealed to Hicks and his fellow Quakers both for its gentle images and its message of a peaceful world: "The wolf also shall dwell with the lamb, and the leopard shall lie down with the kid, and the calf and the young lion and fatling together; and a little child shall lead them." Hick's lion, endowed with sharp, meat-tearing teeth, is offered hay to eat.

It is rarely noticed that in many versions of the painting, Hicks included a vignette of William Penn's treaty with a local tribe of Native Americans. This seems a strange insertion of reality into an otherwise wholly unnatural image. We are still in the world of symbol, however, for it was Penn's view that by introducing Quakerism into Pennsylvania, he was bringing about a peaceable kingdom on earth. Indeed, the little child of Isaiah plays an additional role beyond leading all of nature into peaceful co-existence: he also represents the New World's liberty and freedom from autocratic oppression.

Careful study of the versions of *The Peaceable Kingdom* leads to the conclusion that Hicks wrestled with the contradictions between his idyllic symbols and the real state of nature. In the earliest of his painting, wild animals appear domesticated and living as if in loving-kindness. Their faces, however, seem to express puzzlement about their circumstances, as if they are aware that, in having been forced to cast aside instinct, they are not behaving as animals behave. As one version of *The Peaceable Kingdom* succeeds another, animals that had been huddled in companionship become more dispersed, the tree under which they are gathered begins to look as if it has been blasted by storm, and the child recedes from prominence. Hicks gradually paints more realistic animals, beasts that snarl and raise their claws with apparent intent to strike. The animals become visibly older and tired looking, their eyes sunken, their whiskers whitened, their expressions saddened. Their docility appears to come more from fatigue than from the blessing of peace. In the last painting Hicks' images suggest dashed hopes, as if he had come to realize that the idyllic state is unattainable and perhaps undesirable.

We studied Hicks' paintings because we had noticed that the words from Isaiah that inspired them have been employed by Ingrid Newkirk and other animal rights leaders to express the far-distant goal of their movement. We were surprised by the progression—from the idyllic to the skeptical—that careful examination revealed. This progression mirrors our conviction that the animal rights movement is more a violation of nature than a realization of the natural ideal. It has nothing to do with bettering the lives of animals; it has everything to do with marketing an impractical ideology to animal lovers and all people of good will and using violence or the threat of violence in pursuit of impossible and dangerous goals. It identifies targets, creates stories, fabricates facts, and sits by, always ready to take credit for a handful of its extremist believers who engage in "direct action." This is the "dirty little secret" of the animal rights movement.

It also appeared that Hicks' increasing pessimism is not just about the peaceable animal kingdom, but also about human civilization. The vignette of Europeans and Native Americans recedes into the background and, eventually, off the canvas. Perhaps William Penn's dream—the European intrusion in the New World would result in a peaceable kingdom—was turning out to be an illusion.

In human history, good and evil are always and inextricably mixed. Certainly, millions of immigrants have found life, liberty, and pursuit of happiness in the new world. At the same time, Native American populations and cultures have been destroyed, the "garden" of nature has been polluted, and social inequality has raised up new generations aspiring to a greater share in the general well-being.

In the world's ambiguity, however, one group can claim credit for much good. Basic biomedical researchers have made our lives longer and healthier. This group may not be represented in Hicks' gatherings of people who would lead us into the peaceable kingdom, but they belong there. As we have argued again and again in this book, what they have accomplished and what they do today through their humane, compassionate use of animals needs to be told. It should never be kept as a "dirty little secret."

APPENDIX A

TWENTY QUESTIONS

If you skipped the preface and haven't guessed by now, we are convinced that knowledge gained from animal research has extended and improved the quality of human and animal lives. We believe that research animals are valued and treated with the utmost care and compassion. And we fear that in spite of these truths, animal research is becoming a "dirty little secret," public support for it is continuing to decline, and advances in medical knowledge and treatments are in jeopardy.

As we have pointed out, there is a hazy frontier between the concerns of animal welfare advocates and animal rights partisans. In that realm, *bona fide* concerns get mixed up with leading questions that are larded with misrepresentation and insinuation. Our only recourse is to treat all questions as honest questions. We have collected a jumble of such frequently asked questions, and, at the risk of repetition, we try to answer them here.

1. WHY DON'T SCIENTISTS USE THE ALTERNATIVES TO ANIMAL RESEARCH—COMPUTER MODELS, CELL CULTURES, AND EPIDEMIOLOGICAL STUDIES?

There are no alternatives to using animals in research—if by alternatives you mean replacements. Yes, there are computer models, cell cultures, epidemiological studies, and, to expand on the list so popular with animal rightists, new brain-imaging technologies. All of them have been developed by scientists themselves. All have reduced the number of animals used in research.

Only when scientists demonstrate to their IACUCs that they have exhausted the potential of these methods are they allowed to continue their investigations with animal models. Computers can only process, not generate, information about the complicated interactions among cells, tissues, and organs that occur in humans and animals. Cell cultures, of course, originate from animal tissue and, while valuable for studying basic interactions, don't reflect perfectly the responses of a whole animal. Epidemiological studies provide clues to disease, but don't reveal the mechanisms by which infectious agents cause diseases or the means by which drugs act. And brain-imaging technologies still do not achieve the resolution that is necessary to understand molecular activity.

2. ANIMALS AREN'T HUMANS. HOW CAN RESEARCH RESULTS DERIVED FROM ANIMAL RESEARCH BE APPLIED TO HUMANS?

The proof is in the pudding: virtually every major medical advance of the last century is due, in part, to research with animals. For example, much of what we know about the immune system has come from studies with mice, and much of what we know about the cardiovascular system has come from studies with dogs. The fact that a virus called SIV causes an immune-suppressing disease in monkeys, but HIV doesn't, is important to understanding the human immune system and immune-suppressing diseases.

Biomedical research using nonhuman species, also known as comparative medicine, yields results because nature makes use of the same or similar genes, proteins, hormones, and chemicals over and over again, often in new and surprising variations, in different species. Thus, there are both striking similarities and instructive differences between the physiological systems of humans and various species of animals. Studying both the similarities and the differences is crucial to medical advance.

3. WHAT ANIMALS ARE USED IN RESEARCH?

This is a question that we ask students touring the Primate Center. Invariably the first person to shout out an answer tells us that monkeys are the animals used in greatest number. Quiet. A second, more cautious voice says, "Cats." More silence. A third but triumphant voice says that for sure it must be dogs. After that, complete and embarrassed silence.

As a matter of fact, about 95 percent of research animals are rodents—that is, if you don't count fruit flies or zebra fish. Dogs and cats comprise less than one percent, and primates less than one-half of one percent.

4. WHERE DO RESEARCHERS GET ANIMALS?

Rats, mice, and other rodents—the most commonly used animals in research—are bred specifically for research, and scientists purchase them from licensed animal breeders. So also are small numbers of pigs, sheep, and other farm animals. Special rules govern how research institutions obtain dogs, cats, and primates, which together comprise about one percent of research animals. Most primates in the United States are bred specifically for research.

5. AREN'T LOST AND STOLEN PETS USED IN RESEARCH?

Provisions of the Animal Welfare Act, which is diligently enforced by USDA inspectors, guarantee that pet dogs and cats do not accidentally end up as research subjects. Despite frequent, unsubstantiated accusations to the contrary, there is absolutely no evidence to support the claim that millions of dogs and cats are taken from homes and shelters and sold to laboratories. According to the March 1998 issue of the animal activist publication *Animal People*, law enforcement efforts have "virtually halted thefts for laboratory use." No scientist would want to use someone's pet.

6. HOW CAN WE JUSTIFY DOING PAINFUL EXPERIMENTS ON ANIMALS?

Those who work with research animals—scientists, veterinarians, and animal care technicians—care about them. They recognize that using animals in research is a privilege that carries with it the responsibility to treat those animals humanely. In the words of famed heart surgeon Dr. Michael DeBakey:

> These scientists, veterinarians, physicians, surgeons, and others who do research in animal laboratories are as much concerned about the care of the animals as anyone can be. Their respect for the dignity of life and compassion for the sick and disabled, in fact, is what motivated them to search for ways of relieving the pain and suffering caused by diseases. (Hulsey)

Besides the basic humanity of researchers, there is a scientific guarantee that prevents most animal pain: it is in the best interest of science itself to provide good animal care. Scientists know that good science depends on healthy animals. Animals that are hungry or agitated, pained or distressed do not yield useful research data.

One purpose of the IACUC reviews of animal research proposals is to consider the research plans from the animals' point of view. Most of the time an experiment is not painful; when it is, pain-relieving drugs are given as part of the research design. A few experiments do involve painful procedures because pain is being studied or because painkillers would interfere with the research. Strict rules, outlined in chapter 9, govern those experiments.

The only research that is acceptable to scientists is research conducted according to the guidelines of humane and compassionate animal care. That is the middle ground between animal cruelty and animal rights extremism. The majority of people who want health advances and also want animals treated humanely support this middle ground.

7. WHAT HAPPENS TO ANIMALS ONCE AN EXPERIMENT IS COMPLETED?

Many research animals must be euthanized to obtain tissue for pathological evaluation and for use in laboratory studies. Euthanasia is the act of inducing a humane death. Research institutions follow the guidelines for euthanasia of the American Veterinary Medical Association.

Those animals involved in experiments that do not require tissue for pathological evaluation may be included in additional experiments. However, except in rare circumstances, federal regulations do not allow an animal to be used in more than one major surgical procedure.

8. DO WE HAVE THE RIGHT TO EXPERIMENT ON ANIMALS? WHAT ABOUT THEIR RIGHTS?

It is important to distinguish between animal rights and animal welfare. The scientific community supports animal welfare, which means guaranteeing the health and well-being of research animals. Most of us accept the idea that farmers, pet owners, zookeepers, and research scientists have the right to use animals for food, companionship, education, and medical knowledge as long as they treat them humanely.

Humans have rights because we also take responsibility for our actions. Not the least responsibility is that of caring for animals in a humane and compassionate way. Animals don't bear responsibilities, and for that reason they are not considered to have rights in the strict sense of the word. When we say that they have a "right" to be treated well, we really mean that we have an obligation to treat them well.

The right to use animals in research—always humanely and compassionately—carries with it an ethical and legal obligation. We are bound to relieve both humans and animals from the specter of disease and suffering, and nearly every major advance of the twentieth century in human and veterinary medicine has depended largely on research with animals. Our best hope for developing preventions, treatments, and cures for diseases such as Alzheimer's, AIDS, cancer, and many animal diseases will also involve biomedical research with animals.

According to the Nuremburg Code, drawn up after World War II, experiments on humans "should be designed and based on the results of animal experimentation" (Nuremburg Code). The Declaration of Helsinki, adopted in 1964 by the Eighteenth World Medical Assembly and revised in 1975, also states that medical research on human subjects "should be based on adequately performed laboratory and animal experimentation" (Declaration of Helsinki).

9. WHY DO VETERINARIANS, WHO ARE SUPPOSED TO CARE FOR SICK ANIMALS, DO EXPERIMENTS ON THEM?

Indeed, laboratory-animal veterinarians choose their profession out of concern for animals. They want to guarantee that research animals are treated humanely. The growing field of laboratory-animal medicine has refined the care and treatment of laboratory animals, making research animals healthier and more comfortable.

Another motivation is that they realize that results of animal research improve the health of animals as well as humans.

10. WHAT'S IN IT FOR THE ANIMALS?

Many of the advances in veterinary medicine are the direct result of research with animals. Veterinarians routinely save the lives of dogs by administering the parvovirus vaccine, developed in animal research. Pacemakers for both humans and animals were developed through research on dogs. Research in reproductive physiology on animals has helped save certain species from extinction.

Even laboratory animals benefit from the research being done with them. Beneficiaries of health care and protection from predators, they often live longer than their cousins in natural habitats. Their deaths, whether for experimental or humane reasons, occur under anesthesia and never involve the cruelty that characterizes the natural world.

11. WHY ARE INCREASING NUMBERS OF ANIMALS SACRIFICED FOR RESEARCH, ESPECIALLY FOR REPETITIVE EXPERIMENTS?

The number of animals used in research has actually decreased in the past twenty years, largely due to nonanimal methods used in early stages of drug testing. Best estimates for the reduction in the overall use of animals in research range from 20 to 50 percent. The number of cats used in research has dropped 66 percent since 1967.

Repetition of some experiments must occur for a variety of scientific reasons. One experiment alone does not establish a fact; validation of the data in subsequent experiments is critical to minimize or discover potential error. Also, even the slightest change in variables such as dosage, temperature, and weight requires "repetition" of an experiment under the new conditions.

12. IS BASIC RESEARCH REALLY NECESSARY TO MEDICAL ADVANCES?

Basic animal research produces the information that drug companies use to create new medicines and devices. Sometimes diseases are noted in naturally sick animals. Sometimes, following a careful scientific hunch, researchers make a model; that is, an animal that is altered to manifest a disease. The proof that lack of insulin caused diabetes, for instance, came from removing the (insulin-producing) pancreas from dogs. To confirm that they understand the basis of the disease correctly, researchers then repair the injury or disease they have created. To continue with our example, they gave injections of insulin to a diabetic dog, and the diabetes was cured. Later, other researchers improve the drug, just as contemporary scientists have devised insulin formulations that can be injected less frequently and insulin that has been cloned from human insulin. At each stage, after the drug is designed, it is tested in animals and then humans.

It is beyond question that the first step of basic animal research produces information that has extended our lifespan and improved the quality of life for humans *and* for animals.

13. DO ANIMAL RIGHTISTS HAVE SOME VALID POINTS TO MAKE?

Those who seek to end animal research—either because they choose to reject its well-established validity and usefulness or because they believe the life of a rat is equal in importance to the life of a human child—contribute little to the progress in laboratory animal welfare. In fact, they have gone to shocking lengths to subvert medical and scientific progress. University laboratories have been broken into, animals stolen, and years of research data destroyed. One animal rights leader, Tom Regan, put the new animal rights agenda in a pithy rallying cry: "It's not bigger cages we want [for laboratory animals], but empty cages!" (Regan 1998).

14. HAVE ANIMAL RIGHTISTS HELPED IMPROVE THE SITUATION FOR RESEARCH ANIMALS?

This question brings to mind two observations on human behavior: first, human beings are always trying to make things better, whether it is the safety devices in cars, teaching methods in schools, treatments in hospitals, or the care of animals.

Second, everyone likes to get the credit for the advances. In terms of care of laboratory animals, the credit for making things go better belongs to the professional associations of veterinarians and animal care personnel who have been at work for years on ways to improve the conditions of animals in their care. Some animal rightists like to think that they are responsible for advances, but they understand little about the basis of improving life for the animals.

15. DOESN'T IT SEEM THAT MORE AND MORE AMERICANS OPPOSE ANIMAL RESEARCH?

The vast majority of Americans support improving human and animal health through the responsible and humane use of animals in medical and scientific research. And most Americans love animals. The two concepts are not mutually exclusive—when you know the facts. Though it isn't easy to reconcile our love and appreciation for animals and the essential need for animal research, knowing that the animals are treated responsibly, ethically, and as humanely as possible strengthens our understanding and respect for animal research.

16. ISN'T IT TRUE THAT A GROWING NUMBER OF DOCTORS ARE QUESTIONING WHETHER ANIMAL RESEARCH IS AN EFFICIENT WAY TO DO MEDICAL RESEARCH?

Contrary to a common public perception, the American medical community is not divided over the use of animals in biomedical research. Surveys taken between 1948 and 1998 show that physician support for animal research has remained constant at about 97 percent.

17. WHAT IS THE NEED FOR TESTING CONSUMER PRODUCTS ON ANIMALS IF SOME COMPANIES DON'T DO THAT?

Some companies promote their products with a misleading statement that the products have not been tested on animals. Although the particular products being advertised in this way might not have been tested, such types of products have been tested by other companies, or their ingredients have been tested for safety on animals.

18. HAS ANYTHING REALLY VALUABLE COME FROM PRIMATE RESEARCH?

When those of us born before 1950 were in high school, we couldn't go swimming in public pools during the summer for fear of contracting and being paralyzed by the poliovirus. Then, in 1956, the Salk vaccine removed this scourge from American life. Today, thanks to the availability of monkey models and decades of basic research and vaccine trials, few young people have even heard of polio. It is important to remember that basic research on polio, relying heavily on monkeys, began in the early 1900s. It takes a long time to get a vaccine or a treatment or a medication from the scientist's lab bench to the patient's bedside. Recent advances are giving hope to AIDS and leukemia patients and those who have relatives with Alzheimer's, other neurodegenerative diseases, diabetes, and cancer.

19. WHAT MAKES MONKEYS SO VALUABLE TO RESEARCH?

Because rhesus monkeys share many characteristics of reproduction with humans, including the twenty-eight-day menstrual cycle, they are very valuable to studies in basic physiology that are necessary to develop contraceptive strategies having fewer health risks than current birth control methods. The surgeries involved in these studies are identical to those performed for women. They are conducted under the same conditions of anesthesia and postoperative pain relief. The only difference is that women sign consent forms, while monkeys and their well-being are protected by IACUC deliberations. This committee makes certain that the research is scientifically necessary and not painful to the monkeys.

20. WHAT HEALTH PROBLEMS COULD BE SOLVED WITH PRIMATE RESEARCH?

There is an essential need for nonhuman primates, mainly rhesus monkeys, in the study of arteriosclerosis, contraception, women's health issues such as depression associated with reproductive events, reproductive disorders, Alzheimer's, Parkinson's disease, and infectious diseases such as viral hepatitis and AIDS.

APPENDIX B

RESOURCES

We live in an Internet world. The list below provides URL links to groups on both sides of the fence: those supporting animal research and those in (sometimes violent) opposition. Users should be aware that it is possible to capture the IP address of those viewing sites and even download programs or otherwise violate expectations of privacy. Individuals who use this list and are unfamiliar with Internet security measures should consult experts in this area prior to using any sites.

RESEARCH ADVOCACY GROUPS

AIDS Education Global Information System, http://www.aegis.com/

Americans for Medical Progress, http://www.amprogress.org/

American Health Assistance Foundation, http://www.ahaf.org/

Biomedical Research Alliance of New York, http://www.brany.com/

California Biomedical Research Association, http://www.ca-biomed.org/

Connecticut United for Research Excellence (CURE), http://www.curenet.org/

European Biomedical Research Association, http://www.ebra.org/

Federation of American Societies for Experimental Biology, http://www.faseb.org/

Foundation for Biomedical Research, http://www.fbresearch.org/

Funding First/Lasker Foundation, http://www.laskerfoundation.org/about/ffirst.html

Massachusetts Society for Medical Research, http://www.msmr.org/

Michigan Society for Medical Research, http://www.mismr.org/

National Association for Biomedical Research, http://www.nabr.org/

New Jersey Association for Biomedical Research, http://www.njabr.org/

Northwest Association for Biomedical Research, http://www.nwabr.org/

Ohio Scientific Education and Research Association, http://www.osera.org/

Pennsylvania Society for Biomedical Research, http://www.psbr.org/

Public Responsibility in Medicine and Research, http://www.primr.org/

Research! America, http://www.researchamerica.org/

Southwest Association for Education in Biomedical Research (SWAEBR), http://www.swaebr.org/

Southwest Foundation for Biomedical Research, http://www.sfbr.org/

States United for Biomedical Research (SUBR), http://statesforbiomed.org/

Texas Society for Biomedical Research, http://www.tsbr.org/

Washington Association for Biomedical Research (name changed to NWABR in 2003: Northwest Association for Biomedical Research), http://www.nwabr.org/

Wisconsin Association for Biomedical Research & Education, http://www.wabre.org/

ANIMAL WELFARE GROUPS AND AGENCIES

Animal Welfare Information Center (USDA), http://www.nal.usda.gov/awic/

National Animal Interest Alliance, http://www.naiaonline.org/

National Institutes of Health Office of Extramural Research Office of Laboratory Animal Welfare, http://grants.nih.gov/grants/funding/SBIRConf2000/OLAW/

Scientists Center for Animal Welfare, http://www.scaw.com/

Universities Federation for Animal Welfare (UFAW), http://www
.ufaw.org.uk/
University of California (Davis) Center for Animal Welfare, http://
animalwelfare.ucdavis.edu/

ALTERNATIVES TO ANIMAL RESEARCH

Alternatives to Animal Testing/National Library of Medicine/NIH,
http://sis.nlm.nih.gov/
Alternatives to Animal Testing on the Web (ALTWEB Johns Hopkins), http://altweb.jhsph.edu/
Interagency Coordinating Committee on the Validation of Alternative Methods (CCVAM), http://iccvam.niehs.nih.gov/
Institute for In Vitro Studies, http://www.iivs.org/
Johns Hopkins Center for Alternatives to Animal Testing (CAAT),
http://caat.jhsph.edu/
University of California Center for Animal Alternatives, http://
www.vetmed.ucdavis.edu/Animal_Alternatives/main.htm

GOVERNMENT, REGULATORY
& ACCREDITING AGENCIES

Association for Assessment and Accreditation of Laboratory Animal
Care (AALAC), http://www.aaalac.org/
Animal and Plant Health Inspection Service (USDA), http://www
.aphis.usda.gov/
Food and Drug Administration, http://www.fda.gov/
Institute for Laboratory Animal Research/National Academy of
Sciences, http://dels.nas.edu/ilar/
Office of Laboratory Animal Welfare/NIH, http://grants.nih.gov/
grants/olaw/olaw.htm
National Institutes of Health, http://www.nih.gov/
National Cancer Institute, http://www.nci.nih.gov/
National Center for Research Resources, http://www.ncrr.nih.gov/
World Health Organization, http://www.who.int/en/

INDUSTRY GROUPS

Center for Consumer Freedom, http://www.consumerfreedom
.com/
Fur Commission USA, http://www.furcommission.com/

PROFESSIONAL AND SCIENTIFIC RESOURCES

American College of Laboratory Animal Medicine (ACLAM), http://www.aclam.org/index.html

Association of American Medical Colleges, http://www.aamc.org/start.htm

Guide for the Care and Use of Laboratory Animals, http://www.nap.edu/readingroom/books/labrats/

Institutional Animal Care and Use Committees, http://www.iacuc.org/

IACUC Guidebook, http://grants.nih.gov/grants/olaw/GuideBook.pdf

Lab Animal (peer-reviewed journal), http://www.labanimal.com/

Net Vet: Veterinary Government and Law Resources, http://netvet.wustl.edu/law.htm

Public Health Service Policy on Humane Care and Use of Laboratory Animals, http://grants.nih.gov/grants/olaw/references/phspol.htm

PATIENT GROUPS

Patient's Voice for Medical Advance (UK), http://www.patient.co.uk/showdoc/27000089/

RESEARCH FACILITIES

ALSAC-St. Jude Children's Research Hospital, http://www2.stjude.org/

Armed Forces Institute of Pathology (AFIP), http://www.afip.org/

California National Primate Research Center, http://www.crprc.ucdavis.edu/index.html

Duke University Primate Center, http://www.duke.edu/web/primate/index.html

Harvard Medical School/New England National Primate Research Center, http://www.hms.harvard.edu/nerprc/

Iowa State University Laboratory Animal Resources, http://www.lar.iastate.edu/

Laboratory Animal Research Center, http://www.rockefeller.edu/

Oregon National Primate Research Center, http://onprc.ohsu.edu/

University of Colorado Health Sciences Center, http://www.uchsc.edu/animal/

University of Michigan Unit for Laboratory Animal Medicine, http://www.ulam.umich.edu/
University of Nebraska Animal Care and Use Program, http://www.unmc.edu/Education/Animal/animalca.htm
University of Texas- Austin Animal Resources Center, http://www.unmc.edu/Education/Animal/animalca.htm
University of Texas—M. D. Anderson Cancer Center, Dept. of Veterinary Medicine and Surgery, http://www3.mdanderson.org/~vetmed/
Walter Reed Army Institute of Research, http://www.wrair.army.mil/
Wisconsin National Primate Research Center, http://www.primate.wisc.edu/
Yerkes National Primate Research Center (Emory University), http://www.emory.edu/WHSC/YERKES/

PUBLIC VIEWS OF SCIENCE

Engaging Science: Thoughts, Deeds, Analysis and Action, published by the Wellcome Trust, features essays from leading researchers, practitioners, and commentators that discuss public attitudes toward science, the role of media in public engagement, the scientists' perspective, implications for education, linking the public to policy making, and the role of campaigning groups. To download individual chapters, http://www.wellcome.ac.uk/doc_WTX032706.html.

STUDENT SITES

Animals in Research and Education, http://opa.faseb.org/pages/PublicEducators/animalresearch.htm
Animals in Science (Minnesota AALAS), http://www.ahc.umn.edu/rar/MNAALAS/
Federation of American Societies for Experimental Biology (FASEB), http://www.faseb.org/
CityLab, http://www.bumc.bu.edu/Departments/HomeMain.asp?DepartmentID=285

The Electronic Zoo, http://netvet.wustl.edu/ssi.htm
Healthy Animals, http://www.ars.usda.gov/is/np/ha/
U.S. Department of Agriculture/Agricultural Research Service, http://www.ars.usda.gov/main/main.htm
Kids 4 Research, http://www.kids4research.org/
NetVet Animal Resources, http://netvet.wustl.edu/
OSERA Kids (Ohio Scientific Education & Research Association), http://www.osera.org/kids.htm

ANIMAL RIGHTS GROUPS

American Anti-Vivisection Society, http://www.aavs.org/
Americans for Medical Advancement, http://www.curedisease.com/
Animal Legal Defense Fund, http://www.aldf.org/
Animal Liberation Front (ALF), http://www.animalliberationfront.com/
Humane Society of the United States (HSUS), http://www.hsus.org/
In Defense of Animals (IDA), http://www.idausa.org/
National Anti-Vivisection Society, http://www.navs.org/
People for the Ethical Treatment of Animals (PeTA), http://www.peta.org/
Physicians Committee for Responsible Medicine (PCRM), http://www.pcrm.org/
Stop Animal Exploitation Now (SAEN), http://www.all-creatures.org/saen/
Stop Huntingdon Animal Cruelty (SHAC), http://www.shac.net/

NOTES

CHAPTER 3

1. From this basic research, Taub went on to develop techniques, collectively called constraint-induced (CI) movement therapy, which have proven effective for thousands of patients in increasing movement after stroke and other neurological injuries. In 2003, CI therapy was named by the Society for Neuroscience as one of the top ten Translational Neuroscience Accomplishments of the twentieth century.

CHAPTER 5

1. Ringach has not responded to media requests for confirmation of the existence and contents of the email.

CHAPTER 6

1. This claim, recorded by University of Mississippi pharmacologist Robert Speth during a debate in 1996, appears to have been modified by Dr. Buyukmihci. On a Web site available in 2002, we found the qualifier "initially" in this statement: "In addition, many of the great medical advances such as penicillin, the X-ray, and numerous others came from work which did not *initially* involve nonhuman animals" (emphasis added). The article and Web site (Nedim C. Buyukmihci, "Ethical and practical concerns for the use of nonhuman animals in research," http://www.avar.org/research.html) appear to have been taken down.

WORKS CITED

We hope that the Web sites listed in Appendix B provide useful starting points for getting acquainted with the animal rights movement and its threat to human health. The list of readings below, which include only works cited in this book, does not at all cover the vast literature of animal rights and animal research, but it should allow the reader to check on our sources.

ABC. Bob Barker donates $1 million to Northwestern. March 23, 2005. http://abclocal.go.com/wls/story?section=News&id=2902311.

ActivistCash.com [1]. Craig Rosebraugh. http://www.activistcash.com/biography.cfm/bid/2743.

ActivistCash.com [2]. Quotes. http://www.activistcash.com/organization_quotes.cfm/oid/408.

ActivistCash.com [3]. Overview. http://www.activistcash.com/organization_overview.cfm/oid/408.

ActivistCash.com [4]. Overview. http://www.activistcash.com:80/organization_overview.cfm/oid/23.

Allan, Carrie. What is a word. HSUS Resource Library. December 20, 2000. http://www.animalsheltering.org/resource_library/magazine_articles/nov_dec_2000/whats_in_a_word.html.

Americans for Medical Progress [1]. AMP News Service special report: At the Animal Rights 2001 Conference. Email posted from amp@amprogress.org. July 10, 2001.

Americans for Medical Progress [2]. AMP news: LSR/HLS to begin trading on NYSE/Arca. Email posted from amp@amprogress.org. December 22, 2006.

Animal Liberation Front. Monumental animal liberation front actions—United States. http://www.animalliberationfront.com/ALFront/Actions-USA/alfusa.htm.

Asthana, Anushka, Jamie Doward, and Diane Taylor. Death threat for teenage animal test supporter. *Guardian*, February 26, 2006.

http://www.guardian.co.uk/print/0,,329421232-110650,00
.html.

Avgerinos, Zoy. Animal cruelty caught on tape. CBS Worldwide. September 7, 2000. http://portland.indymedia.org/en/2005/ 08/323248.shtml?discuss.

BBC [1]. Arsonists target lab staff. August 28, 2000. http://news .bbc.co.uk/1/hi/uk/899764.stm.

BBC [2]. Banned activist will give speech. October 26, 2004. http://news.bbc.co.uk/2/hi/uk_news/3599858.stm.

BBC [3]. The world at one. BBC Radio 4. August 27, 2004. http://www.furcommission.com/debate/words87.htm.

BBC [4]. Clear threats to new Oxford lab. BBC News. May 18, 2006. http://news.bbc.co.uk/1/hi/uk/4992434.stm.

BBC [5]. NYSE "caved in" on lab firm float. BBC News. October 27, 2005. http://news.bbc.co.uk/2/hi/business/4381374.stm.

Bai, Matt. Breaking the cages. *Newsweek*, September 29, 1997. http://www.adherents.com/misc/animal_rights.html.

Barnard, Jeff. Animal Liberation Front arsonists sentenced to 12 years. *Oregonian*, May 24, 2007. http://seattletimes.nwsource .com/html/localnews/2003721517_ecosentence25m.html.

Barnard, Neal D. Doctors sue NIH over controversial cat experiments. PCRM. December 26, 2001. http://www.pcrm.org/ news/issues011226.html.

Barnard, Neal D., and Stephen R. Kaufman. Animal research is wasteful and misleading. *Scientific American* 276, no. 2 (1997): 80–82.

Baxter, Jim. Intimidation and harassment. *Chemistry and Industry* 3 (2001): 70–71.

Bend Weekly. Defendants plead guilty to arson and conspiracy charges in ELF & ALF crimes, some in central Oregon. July 21,2006. http://www.bendweekly.com/Local-News/536.html.

Berkowitz, P. Other people's mothers. *New Republic* 4, no. 434 (2000): 27–37.

Better Business Bureau. BBB wise giving report for People for the Ethical Treatment of Animals. April 2006. http://charityreports .give.org/Public/Report.aspx?CharityID=1160.

Berman, Richard. Animal groups callous, not cute. *USA Today*, April 15, 2003. http://www.usatoday.com/news/opinion/editorals/ 2003-04-15-berman_x.htm.

Bite Back. http://www.directaction.info/news_feb01_06.htm.

Blair, Linda. *Steppin' Out.* http://www.reason.com/news/show/30950.html.

Bliss, Michael. *The discovery of insulin.* Toronto: McClelland & Stewart, 1982.

Blumberg, Mark S. The animal zealotry that destroyed our lab. *Washington Post,* July 17, 2005.

Bogle, Rick [1]. Dora E. Angelaki: The "Little Angel" of St. Louis. http://www.primatefreedom.com/essays/doraangelaki.html.

Bogle, Rick [2]. Email message to author. October 3, 2003.

Bogle, Rick [3]. Email message to author. September 24, 2003.

Bogle, Rick [4]. Email message to Gary Granger. September 26, 2003.

Boston Animal Defense League. Operation: Knockout mission accomplished.http://boston.animaldefense.info/?sec=news& nwi=140.

Boston Herald, August 25, 2002. http://www.activistcash.com/organization_overview.cfm/oid/408.

Botting, Jack H. Burying the penicillin myth. *Research Defence Society News,* July 1995.

Botting, Jack H., and Adrian R. Morrison [1]. Animal research is vital to medicine. *Scientific American* 276 (1997): 83–85.

Botting, Jack H., and Adrian R. Morrison [2]. Unscientific American animal rights or wrongs. *Biomednet,* February 20, 1998. http://iinet.net.au/~rabbit/unscian.htm.

Brown, Chip. She's a portrait of zealotry in plastic shoes. *Washington Post,* November 13, 1983, B1–10.

Budiansky, Stephen [1]. *The covenant of the wild: Why animals chose domestication.* New York: William Morrow and Company, 1992.

Budiansky Stephen [2]. If a lion could talk. New York: Free Press, 1998.

CBS [1]. Bob Barker recovering. September 17, 1999. http://www.cbsnews.com/stories/1999/09/17/entertainment/main62691.shtml.

CBS [2]. FBI tracks ecoterrorists. *60 Minutes.* January 11, 2001. http://www.cbsnews.com/stories/2001/01/11/60minutes/printable263478.shtml.

CBS [3]. Interview with ALF cell member. *60 Minutes.* November 13, 2005. http://www.cbsnews.com/stories/2005/11/11/60minutes/main1041047.shtml.

Canada Free Press. True green report: Rats before human life. February 17, 2003. http://www.canadafreepress.com/2003/tgr 021703.htm.

Capaldo, Theodora. ESEC responds: Depicts animal advocates as "lunatic science-hating fringe." *USA Today*, December 10, 1999.

Carlson, Peter. Michele Rokke's undercover life for animal rights. *Washington Post*, January 3, 1998. http://www.junkscience .com/news/peta.html.

Carmichael, Mary. Atkins under attack: The carb wars have gone guerilla. Inside the release of the diet doc's medical info—and the group responsible. *Newsweek*, February 23, 2004. http://www .newsweek.com/id/53175.

Carnell, Brian [1]. Americans for Medical Progress on Animal Rights 2001. A special report of Americans for Medical Progress at the 2000 Animal Rights Conference. July 7, 2001. http:// www.animalrights.net/archives/year/2001/000134.html.

Carnell, Brian [2]. Federal agents arrest seven activists in four states. Animal Rights.net. June 2, 2004. http://www.animalrights.net/ archives/year/2004/000237.html.

Carruthers, P. *The animals issue.* Cambridge: Cambridge University Press, 1992.

Caton, Josh. Cat AIDS researcher says Ohio State didn't back him. *Other Paper*, June 20, 2002.

Cavalieri, Paola, and Peter Singer, eds. *The Great Ape Project.* New York: St. Martin's, 1993.

Center for Consumer Freedom. PCRM week: The AMA's admonishments of PCRM. April 14, 2005. http://www.consumerfreedom .com/news_detail.cfm/headline/2786.

Chicago Daily Herald. True green report: Rats before human life. June 16, 2002. http://canadafreepress.com/2003/tgr021703 .htm.

Close, Elaine. SARS vaccine question. Independent Media Center. May 11, 2003. http://portland.indymedia.org/en/2003/05/ 264328.shtml.

Cohen, Andrew Neal. Weeding the garden. *Atlantic Monthly* 270, no. 5 (November 1992): 76–86.

Colen, B. D. Of fanged bunny huggers. *New York Newsday*, June 23, 1992.

Committee on the National Needs for Research in Veterinary Science, National Research Council. *Critical needs for research in veterinary science.* National Academies, 2005.

Cook, John. Thugs for puppies. Salon.com. February 7, 2006. http://www.salon.com/mwt/feature/2006/02/07/thugs_puppies/index_np.html.

Costello, Michael. Zero tolerance for PeTA. *Lewiston Morning Tribune*, October 10, 2003. http://michaelcostello.blogspot.com/2003/10/zero-tolerance-for-peta.html.

Crawley, Michael. Kenya mounts a game plan to cut elephant counts. *Christian Science Monitor*, September 12, 2001.

Cronon, William. The trouble with wilderness; Or, getting back to the wrong nature. In *Uncommon ground: Toward reinventing nature*, ed. William Cronon, 49–90. New York: W. W. Norton, 1995.

Dawdy, Philip [1]. The spy who loved monkeys. *Willamette Week*, February 6, 2001. http://www.wweek.com/html2/leada020601.html.

Dawdy, Philip [2]. Fractured hopes. *Willamette Week*, February 21, 2001. http://willametteweek.com/html2/newsbuzz022101.html.

Dawkins, Marian Stamp. The scientific basis for assessing suffering in animals. In *In defense of animals*, ed. Peter Singer 26–39. New York: Basil Blackwell, 1985.

DeBakey, Michael. Notable quotes. http://www.swaebr.org/cfaar/Animal_Research_Database.htm#1.5.

Declaration of Helsinki. Recommendations guiding medical doctors in biomedical research involving human subjects. World Medical Association, 1975. http://ethics.iit.edu/codes/coe/world.med.assoc.helsinki.1975.html.

Demopoulos, Katherine. Oxford prepares for first pro-vivisection protest. *Guardian Unlimited*, February 24, 2006. http://education.guardian.co.uk/businessofresearch/story/0,,1717340,00.html.

Dennis, Robert. Doctoral students & post docs. http://www-personal.umich.edu/~bobden/bob_contact_info.html.

Donohue, Bill. Craig Rosebraugh's war. *Inc.com*, October 2005. http://www.inc.com/magazine/20051001/rosebraugh.html.

Dvorak, Todd. Attacks on animal research labs bring economic and human costs. *Waterloo Cedar Falls Courier*, July 1, 2005. http://www.wcfcourier.com/articles/2005/06/25/news/breaking_news/doc42bd416760793657839944.txt.

Economist. Sympathy for activism is on the wane. July 27, 2006. http://www.economist.com/world/britain/displaystory.cfm?story_id=7226037.

Elias, Paul. Animal rights extremism FBI's top domestic terrorism priority. *Associated Press*, June 21, 2005. http://www.mercedes shop.com/shopforum/archive/index.php/t126674.html.

FBI Norfolk. Case ID #266A-NF-NEW. May 10, 2001.

Finkelstein, Susan I. High noon for animal rights law: The coming showdown between pet owners and guardians. *Bellweather Magazine*. Summer 2003.

Foundation for Biomedical Research [1]. Historical myths about animal research. http://www.fbresearch.org/education/History Myths.htm.

Foundation for Biomedical Research [2]. The "nonanimal" method that wasn't. *FBR Facts* V, no. 6 (February 1999).

Foundation for Biomedical Research [3]. Extremists succeed in campaign of intimidation: All of us stand to lose. 2006. http://www.fbresearch.org/Journalists/Releases/Extremist2006.htm.

Florey, Howard. The advance of chemotherapy by animal experiment. *Conquest* 41 (January 1953): 4–14.

Francione, Gary. *Introduction to animal rights: Your child or the dog.* Philadelphia: Temple University Press, 1995.

Francione, G., and A. Charlton. *Vivisection and dissection in the classroom: A guide to conscientious objection.* Jenkintown, PA: American Anti-Vivisection Society, 1992.

Freeman, Mark. Arson in the name of activism. *Mail Tribune*, February 26, 2006. http://www.mailtribune.com/archive/2006/0226/local/stories/01local.htm.

Friedman, Marc. Defendant Kevin Tubbs' motion for release pending sentencing pursuant to Title 18 U.S.C. §3145. United States District Court for the District of Oregon. January 8, 2007.

French, Richard D. *Antivivisection and medical science in Victorian society.* Princeton, NJ: Princeton University Press, 1975.

Gilmartin, Raymond V. *America's leadership in pharmaceutical research: How can we keep winning?* New York: Merck, 1997.

Goodwin, Jo-Ann. The animals of hatred. *Daily Mail*, October 15, 2003.

Greek C. Ray, and Jean Swingle Greek. *Sacred cows and golden geese: The human cost of experiments on animals.* New York: Continuum International, 2000.

Green, William. Testimony before the U.S. Senate Committee on the Judiciary. May 18, 2004. http://judiciary.senate.gov/testimony.cfm?id=1196&wit_id=3462.

Huntingdon Life Sciences vs. Stop Huntingdon Animal Cruelty. California Court of Appeal, Fourth District, Div. 1 No. D042950. June 1, 2005. http://www.casp.net/shac-1.html.

Heaney, Robert. Statement to the Committee on Education and Workforce Hearings. October 7, 2003. Proceedings available from the National Archive of the United States, Washington, DC

Hearne, V. What's wrong with animal rights? *Harpers* 283, no. 1696 (1991): 59–64. Citation from Jeremy Bentham, *Introduction to the principles of morals and legislation* (New York: Hafner, 1946), 310–11.

Henig, Samantha. UCLA professor stops monkey research in response to pressure from animal rights activists. *Chronicle of Higher Education,* August 10, 2006. http://chronicle.com/daily/2006/08/2006081005n.htm.

Hulsey, Martin G., and Roy J. Martin. The role of animals in nutritional research. *Nutrition Today* 29, no. 5 (1993). http://www.highbeam.com/doc/1G1-14236447.html.

Independent Media Center. Portland's finest. July 31, 2005. http://portland.indymedia.org/en/2005/07/322423.shtml.

Inside Higher Ed. Throwing in the towel. August 22, 2006. http://www.insidehighered.com/news/2006/08/22/animal.

Interview with ALF cell member. *CBS 60 Minutes.* November 13, 2005. http://www.cbsnews.com/stories/2005/11/11/60minutes/main1041047.shtml.

Jamison, Wesley V., and William M. Lunch. Rights of animals, perceptions of science, and political activism: Profile of the American animal rights activist. *Science, Technology and Human Values* 17, no. 4 (Autumn 1992): 438–58.

Jaschik, Scott. Fighting back against extremists. *Inside Higher Ed,* August 28, 2006. http://insidehighered.com/news/2006/08/28/ucla.

JAVMA News. AVMA opposes pet guardianship. July 1, 2003. http://www.avma.org/onlnews/javma/jul03/030701i.asp.

Justice Department. http://www.animalliberationfront.com/Philosophy/AbuseLinked/justiced.htm.

Kaiser, Jocelyn. Activists ransack Minnesota labs. *Science,* no. 284 (April 16, 1999): 410–11.

Kargymm, Darby. Fighting to win: An interview with Craig Rosebraugh. *The "A" Word.* http://www.infoshop.org/inews/article.php?story=03/04/12/1178627&query=rosebraugh.

Key, Jack D., and Alvin E. Rodin. Historical vignette: William Ostler and Arthur Conan Doyle versus the antivivisectionists: Some lessons from history for today. *Mayo Clinic Proceedings*, no. 59 (1984): 186–96.

KGO. Newscast. September 26, 2003. Not archived online.

Kiefer, Heather Mason. Americans unruffled by animal testing. *Gallup Poll*, May 25, 2004. http://www.gallup.com/poll/11767/Americans-Unruffled-Animal-Testing.aspx.

Kim, Gloria. Saving animals they hunt humans. *Macleans*, March 20, 2006. http://www.macleans.ca/article.jsp?content=20060320_123521_123521&source=srch.

Kirwan, William E. Animals are critical for research. *Columbus Dispatch*, June 14, 2002. http://researchnews.osu.edu/archive/kirwanoped.htm.

Kjonaas, Kevin. Animal Rights Convention, 2001, Washington, DC. Speech not in print.

Kleiner, Kurt. Activists up the ante. *New Scientist*, April 17, 1999. http://www.newscientist.com/article/mg16221821.900.html.

Knox, Margaret L. The rights stuff. *Buzzworm: The Environmental Journal*, no. 3 (1991): 31–37.

Leppard, David, and Robert Winnett. Cursing mandarin in knighthood row. *UK Times*, February 15, 2004. http://www.timesonline.co.uk/tol/news/uk/article1020398.ece.

Lessenberry, Jack. Activist devotes life to animal rights. *Blade* (Toledo, OH), June 24, 2001. http://nl.newsbank.com/nlsearch/we/Archives?p_product=TB&p_theme=tb&p_action=search&p_maxdocs=200&s_dispstring=allfields(Yourofsky)&p_field_advanced-0=&p_text_advanced-0=("Yourofsky")&p_perpage=10&p_sort=YMD_date:D&xcal_useweights=no (Article ID: 0106250157).

Liberty Watch. Animal rights? October 17, 2005. http://www.liberty-watch.com/ilwt/051017.php.

Linzey, Andrew. Good causes do not need exaggeration. *Animals' Agenda*, no. 20 (2000): 24–25.

Manning, Elizabeth. Saving the world, one cat at a time. *Willamette Week*, December 3, 1997. http://www.wweek.com/html/cover120397.html.

Mansnerus, Laura. Animal rights activists given prison time. *New York Times*, September 13, 2006. http://www.animalliberationpressoffice.org/media_coverage/20060913_shac7sentenced_ny times.htm.

Marshall, Katherine. Letter to the *Oregonian*. September 6, 2000.

Mathews, Dan. A carrot in cattle country. P*e*TA Blog. http://blog .peta.org/archives/chris/

McArdle, John. Sorting out the facts from the fiction. *Animals' Agenda*, March 1988.

McCabe, Katie. Beyond cruelty. *Washingtonian* 25, no. 5 (1990): 72–77, 185–95.

McKie, Robin [1]. Scientist who stood up to terrorism and mob hate faces his toughest test. *Observer*, September 14, 2003. http://observer.guardian.co.uk/uk_news/story/0,6903,10416 65,00.html.

McKie, Robin [2]. Hundreds shouted at me, "Roll over and die." *Observer*, May 15, 2005. http://observer.guardian.co.uk/ uk_news/story/0,,1484312,00.html.

Mercy for Animals. http://www.mercyforanimals.org/4outrage10 .html.

Michael, Steve. http://theprophetrael.blogspot.com/2006_06_01 _archive.html.

Mitchell, Steve [1]. Animal liberation activists using MySpace to target big pharma." August 8, 2006. http://www.spacewar.com/ reports/Animal_Liberations_Activits_Using_MySpace_To_ Target_Big_Pharma_999.html.

Mitchell, Steve [2]. Animal researcher bows to extremists. UPI, August 8, 2006. Available at http://www.fbresearch.org/ Journalists/Releases/080806.htm.

Morano, Marc. New science curriculum aims to curb "animal rights" influence. CBS News, October 28, 2003. http://www .cnsnews.com/ViewNation.asp?Page=%5CNation%5Carchive% 5C200310%5CNAT20031028a.html.

National Association for Biomedical Research. 2006 Animal Rights conference summary. http://www.nabr.org/pdf/AR06Summary .pdf.

National Research Council—Institute of Laboratory Animal Resources. *Guide for the care and use of laboratory animals*. Washington, DC: National Academy Press, 1996.

Washington City Paper. Nature Conservancy kills kids. July 15, 1994.

Nature Neuroscience [1]. Constitutional protection for animals, vol. 5, no. 611 (2002). http://www.nature.com/neuro/journal/ v5/n7/full/nn0702-611.html.

Nature Neuroscience [2]. Pro-tests for biomedical research, vol. 9, no. 587 (2006). http://www.nature.com/neuro/journal/v9/n5/full/nn0506-587.html.

NBC4 TV. FBI: Animal group leaves "Molotov cocktail" at wrong house. http://www.nbc4.tv/news/9508973/detail.html.

Nelson, J. L. Animals, handicapped children and the tragedy of marginal cases. *Journal of Medical Ethics* 14 (1988): 191–93.

Nuremburg Code. http://www.hhs.gov/ohrp/references/nurcode.htm.

Newbart, Dave. Barker has to bite his lip before giving NU $1 million. *Chicago Sun Times*, March 23, 2005. http://www.findarticles.com/p/articles/mi_qn4155/is_20050323/ai_n13463335.

North American Animal Liberation Front. 2001 year-end direct action report. January 12, 2002.

Northwestern Observer Online. Bob Barker endows animal rights law course. March 31, 2005. http://www.northwestern.edu/observer/issues/2005/03/30/barker.html.

O'Connor, Brian. Grassroots Animal rights conference: Who's in, and who's not. *Animal Crackers*, March 28, 2005. http://brianoconnor.typepad.com/animal_crackers/2005/03/grassroots_anim.html.

O'Neill, Brendan. The truth about "animal rights" terrorism. *Spiked*, August 10, 2006. http://www.spiked-online.com/index.php?/site/article/1463/.

Parker, Laura. When pets die at the vet, grieving owners call lawyers. *USA Today*, March 14, 2005.

Paton, William. *Man and mouse: Animals in medical research*. Oxford: Oxford University Press, 1984.

Paynter, Susan. We can civilly disagree about animal research. *Seattle PI*, October 10, 2003. http://seattlepi.nwsource.com/paynter/143246_paynter10.html.

PCRM. Doctors sue NIH over controversial cat experiments. Contact, Simon Chaitowitz. December 12, 2001. http://www.pcrm.org/news/issues011226.html.

PeTA. How would you feel if a cow ate you? *All-creatures.org*, October 25, 1998. http://www.all-creatures.org/poetry/howwouldyoufeel.html.

Pincock, Stephen. Oxford resumes building animal lab. http://www.the-scientist.com/news/20051202/02/

Pinker, Steven. *The language instinct*. New York: HarperPerennial, 1994.

Primate Freedom Project at UCLA. http://www.uclaprimate freedom.com/. (Web sites targeting Ringach have been taken down.)

Prince, Jeff. Billboard criticizes March of Dimes; group's ad in Dallas denounces animal experiments. *Fort Worth Star-Telegram*, April 1, 2000.

Pristin, Terry. Lab cancels beagle tests. *New York Times*, July 4, 1997.

Psychologists for the Ethical Treatment of Animals. Great Ape Project. http://www.psyeta.org/hia/vol8/tgap.html.

PUBMED. http://www.pubmed.gov.

Regan, Tom [1]. *The case for animal rights*. Berkeley: University of California Press, 1983.

Regan, Tom [2]. The torch of reason, the sword of justice. 1998. http://tomregan-animalrights.com/regan_torch.html.

Reeve, Dana. Past news reports: November 9, 1998. http://www .chrisreevehomepage.com/n-1998.html.

Rivedal, Karen. Wide gulf at animal research debate. *Wisconsin State Journal*, March 23, 2006.

Rosebraugh, Craig [1]. Congressional Testimony, 2002. http:// www.animalrights.net/archives/year/2002/000053.html and http://www.cdfe.org/rosebraugh.htm.

Rosebraugh, Craig [2]. *The logic of political violence: Lessons in reform and revolution*. Portland: Arissa Media Group, 2004.

Russell, Sharon M., and Charles S. Nicoll. A dissection of the chapter "Tools for research" in Peter Singer's *Animal Liberation*. *Proceedings of the Society for Experimental Biology and Medicine*, no. 211 (1996): 109–39.

Sabin, Albert B. Letter to the editor. *Winston-Salem Journal* (North Carolina), March 20, 1992.

Sagan, Carl. In the valley of the shadow. *Parade Magazine*, March 10, 1996, 18–20.

Sapontzis, Steve F. Aping persons—Pro and con. In *The Great Ape Project*, ed. Paola Cavalieri and Peter Singer, 269–77. New York: St. Martin's, 1993.

SHAC [1]. A list of all companies who have dumped Huntingdon. http://www.shac.net/FINANCIAL/dumpedhls.html.

SHAC [2]. Demo in California against HLS supplier Phenomenex. July 2006. http://www.shac.net/ARCHIVES/2006/July/24e .html.

SHAK-UK Listserv. shac-uk@lists.riseup.net.

Singer, Peter [1]. *Animal liberation: A new ethic for our treatment of animals.* New York: Avon Books, 1975.

Singer, Peter [2]. *Animal liberation: A new ethic for our treatment of animals.* 2nd edition. New York: New York Review of Books, 1990.

Singer, Peter [3]. *Practical ethics.* New York: Cambridge University Press, 1993.

Singer, Peter [4]. *Rethinking life and death.* New York: St. Martin's, 1996.

Singer Peter [5]. Sense and sentience: We might not need pig hearts if the ban on human embryo experiments were lifted. *Guardian*, August 21, 1999.

Sokolowski, Jodi. PeTA could lose nonprofit status. *Spokesman Review*, May 28, 2002. http://www.spokesmanreview.com/ news-story.asp?date=052802&ID=s1155092.

Specter, Michael. The extremist. *New Yorker*, April 14, 2003. http://www.michaelspecter.com/ny/2003/2003_04_14_peta .html.

Sperling, Susan. *Animal liberators: Research and morality.* Berkeley: University of California Press, 1988.

Speth, Robert. The penicillin story: The eight mice that roared. *NAIA Bulletin.* http://www.naiaonline.org/body/articles/archives/ inhumn.htm.

Stolberg, Sheryl Gay. Debate over whether to defend animal tests. *New York Times*, July 23, 2002. http://query.nytimes.com/gst/ fullpage.html?sec=health&res=940CE6D71438F930A15754C0 A9649C8B63.

Tannenbaum, Jerrold. Slide lecture delivered at Oregon National Primate Research Center, July 10, 2003. Slides in the possession of lecturer.

Taylor, Michael, and Jim Herron Zamora. Stalking charges against animal rights activists. *San Francisco Chronicle*, May 27, 2004. http://www.sfgate.com/cgibin/article.cgi?f=/c/a/2004/05/ 27/SHAC.TMP.

Teeling-Smith, George. *A Question of balance: The benefits and risks of pharmaceutical innovation.* London: Office of Health Economics, 1980.

Trefil, James. *Are we unique? A scientist explores the unparalleled intelligence of the human mind.* New York: John Wiley and Sons, 1997.

Turville-Heitz, Meg. Violent opposition: Escalating protests may be driving away some researchers. *Scientific American* 282, no. 2 (February 2000): 32.

UCLA Office of Media Relations. Statement regarding animal rights terrorist activities. August 7, 2006. Available from media@support.ucla.edu.

U.S. Department of Justice [1]. Militant animal rights group, six members convicted in campaign to terrorize company, employees and others. http://www.usdoj.gov/usao/nj/press/files/shac0302_r.htm.

U.S. Department of Justice [2]. Report to Congress on the extent and effects of domestic and international terrorism on animal enterprises. http://www.cdfe.org/doj_report.htm.

USA doctors speak out against vivisection. *Los Angeles Times,* April 24, 1991. http://health.org.nz/decl.html.

Walsh, Gareth. Father of animal activism backs monkey testing. *Sunday Times,* November 26, 2006. http://www.timesonline.co.uk/article/0,,2087-2471990,00.html.

Wallen, Kim. Letter. http://lists.envirolink.org/pipermail/ar-news/Week-of-Mon-20030728/004265.html.

Warren, M. A. The case for weak animal rights. In *Animal rights: Opposing viewpoints,* ed. B. Leone and D. Leone, 34–40. San Diego, CA: Greenhaven, 1996.

Washington City Paper, advertisement, July 15, 1994.

Wilson, E. O. *Biophilia.* Cambridge: Harvard University Press, 1984.

Win animal rights. Email posted by "Ima Vegan" (animal_freedom_fighter@yahoo.com). http://centcom@war-online.org and http://war-online.org/.

Wolfe, Alan. *The human difference: Animals, computers and the necessity of social science.* Berkeley: University of California Press, 1993.

Woolf, Jonathon Sprague. The necessity of predators: An evolutionary defense of hunting. *National Animal Interest Alliance News,* November–December 1997. http://www.naiaonline.org/articles/archives/pred1.htm.

WXYZ-TV Action News. May 2, 2003. Available at http://www.furcommission.com/debate/words85.htm.

Ynterian, Pedro A. What we fight for. Great Ape Project, http://
www.greatapeproject.org/news.php. See also http://www.psyeta
.org/hia/vol8/tgap.html and http://www.speakcampaigns.org/
faq.php/

Zeide, Boris. Resolving contradictions in forestry: Back to science.
Forestry Chronicle 77, no. 3 (2001): 973–81.

INDEX

"A" Word, 18
ACT UP, 146–47
Aeschleman Fur Company, 22
AIDS. *See* HIV/AIDS
  feline, 97
Aiken, U.S. District Judge Ann,
  20
ALF. *See* Animal Liberation
  Front (ALF)
Alzheimer's, xi, 2, 123, 162,
  166, 167
American Anti-Vivisection
  Society, 59, 122
American Heart Association,
  147
American Journal of
  Cardiology, 58
American Medical Association
  (AMA), 57
Americans for Medical
  Advancement, 24
Americans for Medical Progress
  (AMP), 61, 72
American Veterinary Medical
  Association (AVMA), 161
Angelaki, Dora E., PhD, 28–29
animal
  activism, xviii, 46
  companions, xix, 60, 104;
    stolen, 159–60
  consciousness, xviii-xix,
    129–30
  euthanasia, 161

extremism, xiii–xiv, xvii–xviii,
    3, 4, 6, 8, 12, 27, 35, 38,
    47, 102, 104, 143; and
    the University of Iowa,
    104
  as guardians, xix, 81, 133
  knowing, xviii
  law, 77–83; animal compan-
    ion jurisdictions, 82; ani-
    mals as property, 79–83;
    Northwestern University
    Law School, 78–79;
    "standing," 79, 81
  liberation, xvii, xix
  pain, 160
  protection, xvii
  research. alternatives,
    157–58; arguments
    against, 63; basic, 112,
    163–64; benefits, xi;
    number of animals
    involved in, 163; and
    pharmaceutical compa-
    nies, 144; and profes-
    sional societies, 144;
    regulation of, 138–42;
    repetition in, 163; and
    universities, 144; war,
    xii–xiii, 11
  rightists, xiv, xix–xx, 7, 8, 13,
    64, 84–90, 109, 111,
    112–15, 117, 121, 123,
    131–37, 149, 158, 164;

and deep ecologists, 90;
and environmentalism,
85–87. *See also* Animal:
law: animals as property
rights, xii–xiii, xvii, 12,
125–35; and distrust of
science, 46; and entertainment, 46; and feminism,
45; and media, 45; and
medical advances, 46; and
mentally impaired, 131;
movement, xii–xiii, xv, 11,
31, 154; movement
adherence, 73; movement
and enivronmentalism,
84; and prosperity, 45;
terrorism in the name of,
8, 101, 106; terrorism
and Ohio State University
in the name of, 97; terrorism and the University of
Iowa in the name of, 105;
terrorism and the
University of Minnesota
in the name of, 105; testing, xvi, 166; transplants,
51; and urbanization, 46;
welfare, xvii, 135–37, 161
Animal Defense League of Los
Angeles, 60
Animal Enterprise Protection
Act, 35, 101
Animal Enterprise Terrorism
Act, 102
Animal Legal Defense Fund
(ALDF), 21, 59
Animal Liberation Front (ALF),
15, 20, 31, 53, 54–57, 85,
100, 147
Animal People, 160

Animal Protection Institute of
America, 59
Animals' Agenda, 90
Animal Welfare Act, 44, 79, 81,
138, 141, 159
Animal Welfare Information
Center, 140
antibiotics, 2
Ape Army, 28, 30
Arizona, University of, 147
Association for the
Accreditation and
Assessment of Laboratory
Animal Care (AAALAC), 6,
27, 141
autism, xi

Baldwin, Alec, 45, 145
Banting, Frederick, 107
Barker, Bob, 77–78, 177
Barnard, Neal, MD, 57–58, 59,
97, 117, 120
and AIDS research, 97
Barnes, Jean, 101, 144
Barron's, 36
Basinger, Kim, 45, 145
Baxter, Jim, 32
Baylor College of Medicine,
Texas Medical Center, 5
beaver populations, 85
Bend Weekly, 20
Benford, M. Sue, 73
Bentham, Jeremy, 48
Berrigan, Daniel, 48
Best, Charles, 107
Better Business Bureau, 54
Bianco, Richard W. *See* Animal:
rights: terrorism and the
University of Minnesota in
the name of
biomedical research. *See* animal
research

bird flu, xi
Bite Back, 34
Blair, Linda, 145
Blakemore, Colin, 111–12
    and terrorism, 104
Bliss, Michael, 122
Bogle, Rick, 27–30, 59, 60
Boston Herald, 32
Boys Town National Research
    Hospital, 21–25
British Heart Foundation, 152
British Medical Association, 42,
    43, 48
Bryan, Stephanie. *See* Juvenile
    diabetes
bubonic plague, xi
Budiansky, Stephen, 88–89
Buyukmihci, Nedim, DVM, 60,
    113

Calendula Café, 16, 19
California condors, 85
Calnan, Jacquie, 72
Canada Free Press, 31
cancer, 2
Capaldo, Theordora, 121
Carnell, Brian, 33
Carrot, Chris P., 68
Cass, Brian, 32
Cavalieri, Paola, 125
CBS 60 Minutes, 14
cell cultures, 4, 6
Center for Consumer Freedom,
    61
Centers for Disease Control,
    138
Chain, Ernest, 114, 116
Charles Schwab, 35
Chicago Daily Herald, 32
Chiron, 34
Christie, U.S. Attorney
    Christopher J., 37

Citibank, 35
Close, Elaine, 60, 121
Coalition Against Animal
    Testing, 60
Coalition Against Primate
    Experimentation and
    Research (CAPER), 60
Coalition to End Primate
    Experimentation, 60, 69
Colen, B. D., 47
Columbia Asset Management,
    34, 38
Columbia University, 77
communication and language,
    130–31
constraint-induced (CI) move-
    ment therapy, 175
Coronado, Rodney, 54
Costello, Michael, 54, 72
*Critical Needs for Research in
    Veterinary Science*, 103
Cronon, William, 89
Cruelty to Animals Act of 1876, 43
Cryptosporidium, 147

Dahmer, Jeffrey, 72
Daily Mail, 56
Dawdy, Philip, 16, 23
Dawkins, Marian Stamp, 132
DeBakey, Michael, 112, 160
Declaration of Helsinki, 162
Declaration on Great Apes,
    126–27
deer overpopulation, 85
Deloitte & Touche, 35
DeRose, Chris, 57
diabetes, 70, 113, 122
diphtheria, 108
Disney World, 72
dissection, 72
    Oregon, 75
    religious objection to, 74

DNA
    human and ape, 128–29
Donlan, Thomas, 36
Down's syndrome, 52
Doyle, Sir Arthur Conan, 43
drug testing, 94–95
Duke University, 4, 77
Dunbar, Bonnie, PhD, 86–87
Duncan, Alan, 32

E magazine, 90
Earth First!, 20
Earth First! journal, 20
Earth Liberation Front (ELF),
    13, 15, 17, 20, 53, 54–57
Ebola, xi, 109
ecology, xx
    deep, xx, 87, 90
    and Native Americans, 85
Economist, 152
Edmunds, Dennis, 74
electro-ejaculation, 6
elephants
    and population stabilization,
        86, 87
ELF. *See* Earth Liberation Front
    (ELF)
Enders, John, 119
English antivivisectionism,
    42–44

Facebook, 72
Fairbanks, Lynn, 100
FBI, 14, 17, 18, 54, 56, 101,
    105
    Joint Terrorism Task Force,
        2, 17, 35
FBR. *See* Foundation for
    Biomedical Research (FBR)
FDA. *See* Food and Drug
    Administration (FDA)
Feinberg, Mark, MD, PhD, 121

FemantleMedia, 77
Ferdin, Pamela, RN, 60
Festing, Simon, 152
Fleming, Alexander, 113–16
Florey, Howard, 113–16, 182
Food and Drug Administration
    (FDA), xvi, 117, 138
Food, Drug, and Cosmetics Act
    of 1962, 117
Fort Worth Star-Telegram, 148
Foundation for Biomedical
    Research (FBR), 61, 62,
    98–99, 101
Foundation to Support Animal
    Protection, 57
Fox, Michael J., 146
Francione, Gary, 74, 111, 127
Franklin, Jon, 46
French, Richard, 44
Friendster, 72
Fund for the Animals, 60
Fur Commission USA, 61

Gandhi, Mahatma, xiv, 8, 14
Geatz, Ron, 84
George Washington University
    School of Medicine, 58, 78
German Basic Law, 109
Goddard College, 14
Gonadotropin Releasing
    Hormone (GnRH), 5
Goodwin, Jo-Ann, 56
Great Ape Project (GAP),
    125–33
Great Swamp National Wildlife
    Refuge, 85
Greek, Jean, 24
Greek, Ray, 24, 121
Grrr! Kids Bite Back, 69
*Guide for the Care and Use of
    Laboratory Animals*, 138

Hamre, Dorothy, 115
Heaney, Robert P., MD, FACP, FACN, 71
hemophilism, 52
Hemstreet, Leslie, 20–21
Hicks, Edward, 153–55
Hillsboro Argus, 20
HIV/AIDS, xi, 2, 48, 70, 93, 94, 97–99, 101, 107, 109, 112, 121, 123, 146, 147, 162, 166, 167
HLS. *See* Huntingdon Life Sciences (HLS)
Hobbs, Tom, Chief Inspector, 33
Holland, Earle, 98
Hope Heart Institute, 149
HSBC, 35
HSUS. *See* Humane Society of the United States (HSUS)
Hubnet Express, 37
Huntingdon Life Sciences (HLS), 30–40

IACUC. *See* Institutional Animal Care and Use Committee (IACUC)
IDA. *See* In Defense of Animals (IDA)
Igniting the Revolution, 15
In Defense of Animals (IDA), 21, 24, 59
independent media, 55
indy media. *See* independent media
influenza mortality rates, 108
Inhofe, Senator James, 15
Institute for Behavioral Research, 44
Institutional Animal Care and Use Committee (IACUC), 123, 138–40

Internal Revenue Service (IRS), 17
invasive species, 84
Iowa Cattlemen's Association, 20
Iowa, University of, 4. *See also* Animal: extremism: and the University of Iowa

Johnson-Brown, Isis, DVM, 24
Jonas, Kevin. *See* Kjonaas, Kevin
Justice Department, 12
juvenile diabetes, 107

Katz, Eliot, 83
Kaufman, Stephen R., MD, 57, 117, 120
Kelsey, Frances, 117
Kerr, Jeffrey, 7, 17, 18
KGO, 34
King, Martin Luther, xiv
Kirwan, William E., 98
Kitchen, Hyram, DVM, 104
Kjonaas, Kevin, 30–40
Kling, Michelle, 148
Koch, Robert, 116
Koop, C. Everett, 123

Lacroix, Charlotte, 82
Lange, Lisa, 18
Last Chance for Animals, 57
Lewiston Morning Tribune, 54
Liberation Collective, 11, 16
Life, 44
life expectancy, 108
Life Sciences Research, Inc. (LSR), 36, 38
Linzey, Rev. Andrew, 44
Logic of Political Violence: Lessons in Reform and Revolution, 14, 18
Low, Walter, 31

LSR. *See* Life Sciences Research, Inc. (LSR)
Lucky the sheepdog, 79

Macleans, 24
Magendie, François, 42
Magnan, Eugene, 42
Maher, Bill, 145
Manning, Elizabeth, 16
March for Animals, 1990, 45, 46
March of Dimes, 147, 148
marmosets, 6
Marsh, Inc., 33, 35
Martin, John, 152
Martin's Act, 42
McArdle, John, PhD, 116
McCartney, Paul, 145
McGee, JoAnn, 22
McInnis, Representative Scott, 13, 17
measles, 108
Medical Research Council, 104
Medical Research Modernization Committee, 57
Mercy for Animals, 96
Merrill Lynch, 35
Michael, Steve, 146–47
Michigan, University of, 5
Midgely, Mary, 45
milk in school lunches, 71
Miller, Anne, 114
Minnesota, University of, 30–31
Moore, Mary Tyler, 145
Morrison, Adrian, DVM, 117
multiple sclerosis, 70
mumps, 108
MySpace, 72

National Association for Biomedical Research (NABR), 61, 62
National Institute of Drug Abuse (NIDA), 96
National Institutes of Health (NIH), xvi, 5, 22, 25, 96–97, 99, 103, 133, 138, 141
National Library of Medicine, 58
National Science Foundation, xvi
Nature Conservancy (TNC), 84, 86, 87
Nelson, James Lindemann, 52
New England Anti-Vivisection Society (NEAVS), 59
Newkirk, Ingrid, 17, 32, 45, 53, 64, 68, 85, 90, 149, 154
New Scientist, 31
New York Newsday, 47
New York Stock Exchange (NYSE), 36
New York Times, 58
Nicoll, Charles, 50
NIH. *See* National Institutes of Health (NIH)
North Carolina State University, 5
Northwestern University, 77, 78
Nuremburg Code, 162
NYSE. *See* New York Stock Exchange

O'Brien, Mike, 32
Obstetrics & Gynecology, American Journal of, 58
Office of Health Economics, 117

Ohio Scientific Education & Research Association, 73
Ohio State University, 97, 98, 99
    College of Veterinary Medicine, 93
ONPRC. *See* Oregon National Primate Research Center (ONPRC)
Operation Fightback, 36
Operation Knockout, 38
Oregon Health and Science University (OHSU), 2, 11
    Public Safety Office, 29
Oregon National Primate Research Center (ONPRC), xii, 2, 8, 11–12, 21, 23, 28, 59
    Division of Animal Care, 21
Oregonian, 21
Oregon, University of, 60
OSU. *See* Ohio State University
Other Paper, 98
Oxford University, 153

Pacheco, Alex, 45, 53, 84
Parkinson's disease, 51, 146, 167
Paton, William, 108
Paynter, Susan, 149
PCRM. *See* Physicians Committee for Responsible Medicine (PCRM)
Peace Corps, 28, 48
Peaceable Kingdom, 153–56
penicillin, 113–16
Pennsylvania Veterinary Medical Association. *See also* Animal: law: animals as property
People for Animal Rights, 60
People for the Ethical Treatment of Animals (PeTA), xii, 2, 4, 7, 13, 17, 18, 21–24, 31, 32, 45, 53–54, 57–60, 64, 68, 69, 71–75, 84, 86, 146, 147
person (hood), xix, 49
pertussis, 108
pet, xix, 159. *See* animal: companions
Physicians Committee for Responsible Medicine (PCRM), 57–59, 60, 71, 97, 147–48
Pinker, Steven, 131
Podell, Michael, DVM, 93–99
polio, xi, 47, 70, 108, 109, 113, 118–21, 166
Primate Freedom Project, 60, 101
Protect Our Earth's Treasures, 96
Pro-Test, 151
Psychologists for the Ethical Treatment of Animals, 127
Public Health Service Act, 138
Pycroft, Laurie, 151–52

Reeve, Christopher, 61, 109, 145–46
Reeve, Dana, 146
Regan, Tom, 133–34, 164
Reines, Brandon, 122
Research Defence Society, 152
Ringach, Dario, 99–102
Robbins, Frederick, 119, 120
Rodent Alliance for Tolerance, 60
Rokke, Michelle, 22, 31
Rosebraugh, Craig, 11, 13–19, 21, 27, 55, 60, 93, 121
Rossell, Matt, 19–27, 59, 83
Royal Canadian Mounted Police, 56

Royal Society for the
    Prevention of Cruelty to
    Animals, 42
rubella, 108
Russell, Sharon, 50

Sabin, Albert, 120
Sagan. Carl, 109
Salk, Jonas, 120, 166
Sapontzis, Steven, 132
Scientific American, 120
Seattle Post Intelligencer, 149
"Setting Fires with Electrical
    Timers: An Earth Liberation
    Front Guide," 15
SHAC 7, 35
SHAC-USA. *See* Stop
    Huntingdon Animal
    Cruelty-USA (SHAC-USA)
Shah, Anuj, 81
Shaklee Corporation, 34
Silverstone, Alicia, 45, 71, 75
Singer, Peter, xvii, xix, 41, 44,
    48–53, 116, 125, 127
    Animal Liberation, 41, 44,
    50
    Rethinking Life and Death,
    131
    *The Great Ape Project:
    Equality Beyond
    Humanity*, 125
Skorton, David. *See* Animal:
    rights: terrorism and the
    University of Iowa in the
    name of
smallpox, xi, 108, 109, 119
Society for Neuroscience, 45
Sokolowski, Jodi, 17
South Florida, University of, 2
SPEAC. *See* Stop Primate
    Experiments at Cambridge
    (SPEAC)
speciesism, xix, 49, 127, 132

Speede, Sheri, DVM, 24
Speth, Robert, 116
Spokane Spokesman Review, 72
Stanford University, 77
States United for Biomedical
    Research, ix
stem cell therapy, 109
Stephens, Inc., 34
Steppin' Out, 145
Stewardship, xx
Stop Huntingdon Animal
    Cruelty-USA (SHAC-USA),
    30–40, 54–56, 60, 100
Stop Primate Experiments at
    Cambridge (SPEAC), 150
Student Organization for
    Animal Rights (SOAR), 31
Students for the Ethical
    Treatment of Animals, 60
Supersize Me, 58
Sweetland, Mary Beth, 21, 22
syphilis, 108

Tannenbaum, Jerrold, 83
Taub, Edward, 44, 45
Tennessee, University of, 104
thalidomide, 116–18
Thompson, Judge Anne E., 36
three Rs (3Rs), 140
TNC. *See* Nature Conservancy
    (TNC)
tool-making, 130
Trefil, James, 130
Troen, Roger, 60
Trull, Frankie, 98, 101
*Truth Behind the Discovery of
    Insulin*, 122
Tubbs, Kevin, 20
tuberculosis, 108

UCLA, 77, 99, 101
    Media Relations Office, 100

United States Department of
    Agriculture (USDA), 6, 24,
    25, 27, 59, 98, 138, 140,
    159
USA Today, 79
utilitarianism, 51

Van Zandt, David, 78
veganism, xx
vegetarianism, xx
Veterinarians for Animal Rights,
    60
violence, 58, 74
vivisection, xviii, 3, 133
*Vivisection and Dissection in the
    Classroom: A Guide to
    Conscientious Objection*, 74
Vlasak, Jerry, MD, 58–59, 60

Walker Brothers Circus, 22
Wallen, Kim, 143
Walsh, Edward, 22, 24

WAR. *See* Win Animal Rights
    (WAR)
Washington Post, 22
Webb, Robin, 150
Weller, Thomas, 119
Willamette Week, 16, 20, 23
Wilson, David, 54
Wilson, E. O., 87
Win Animal Rights (WAR), 38
Wisconsin National Primate
    Research Center (WNPRC),
    30
Wolfe, Alan, 131
Wood, Patty, 146
WXYZ-TV, 74

Yamanouchi Consumer, Inc.,
    34
Yourofsky, Gary, 7, 60
YouTube.com, 73

Zeide, Boris, 88
Zerhouni, Elias, MD, 99